THE NICARAGUAN REVOLUTION

Children from a refugee center give the "V" for victory sign on
July 17, 1979, the day General Anastasio Somoza resigned as
president of Nicaragua and fled the country.

THE NICARAGUAN REVOLUTION

Edited with an Introduction by Pedro Camejo and Fred Murphy

PATHFINDER PRESS, NEW YORK

Acknowledgments

The interview with Jaime Wheelock, "Nicaragua's Plans for Agriculture," is reprinted by permission from the August 24, 1979, *Militant*. The speech by Daniel Ortega, "Nothing Will Hold Back Our Struggle for Liberation," appeared in the October 1, 1979, *Intercontinental Press/Inprecor*. The "Statute on the Rights of Nicaraguans" is reprinted from the September 10, 1979, *Intercontinental Press/Inprecor*. The translation of Fidel Castro's speech, "The Triumph of Nicaraguan Independence," is based on the English text printed in the August 5, 1979, *Granma* Weekly Review. The appendix, "Imperialism Launches Propaganda Drive Against Sandinistas," appeared in the September 3, 1979, *Intercontinental Press/Inprecor*. All items from *Intercontinental Press/Inprecor* are reprinted by permission and copyright © 1979 by *Intercontinental Press*.

Cover photos by Aníbal Yáñez are of the September 14, 1979, rally of 30,000 in Managua in solidarity with Vietnam.

Library of Congress Catalog Card Number 79-55833
ISBN cloth 87348-573-4; paper 87348-574-2
Manufactured in the United States of America

Pathfinder Press
410 West Street
New York, N.Y. 10014

Contents

Introduction

There is a revolution unfolding in Nicaragua today. One of the most brutal dictatorships in Latin America has been overthrown by the workers and peasants, under the leadership of the Sandinista National Liberation Front (FSLN). The imperialist-backed Somoza dictatorship, its army, and its police have been destroyed.

Basing itself on the power of the armed and mobilized masses, the Sandinista leadership has taken a series of radical measures—a deepgoing land reform, nationalization of all the country's banks, seizure of all the property held by the Somoza family and its collaborators, the formation of popular militias and a revolutionary army, and the organization of trade unions and neighborhood committees.

In the course of the brutal civil war that led to the ousting of General Anastasio Somoza Debayle on July 19, 1979, virtually all industry and agriculture in this small, poverty-stricken country was paralyzed and disrupted. The desperate attempt by the U.S.-armed and -financed Nicaraguan National Guard to maintain Somoza in power left a toll of some forty- to fifty-thousand dead and hundreds of thousands homeless. Entire sections of cities were leveled.

Nearly half of Nicaragua's population, including almost half a million children, are suffering from the lack of food, clothing, and shelter. To prevent starvation and disease, more than 300 tons of food and medicine are needed daily.

Responsibility for the destruction and suffering in Nicaragua rests squarely on the U.S. government, which spent tens of millions of dollars installing and supporting Somoza's tyranny. But President Carter and Congress have turned their backs on the new Nicaraguan government's appeal for help. Hundreds of millions of dollars in emergency relief are needed, while Washington stalls on sending even a tiny fraction of this.

An active solidarity campaign among working people throughout the world is urgently needed. The labor movement in Canada, Colombia, and Mexico; the governments of Cuba, the Federal Republic of Germany, and Sweden, to name a few, have sent relief. In the United States, Nicaragua solidarity groups, unions, and churches have begun to collect and send aid. These efforts must be expanded, and the American government must be pressured to provide immediate large-scale aid with no strings attached for rebuilding Nicaragua.

Washington fears the revolutionary steps taken in Nicaragua and their repercussion throughout Latin America. By withholding aid, the U.S. government hopes to pressure the new Government of National Reconstruction to moderate its course. And behind this economic blackmail stands the threat of open military intervention.

Entire units of Somoza's National Guard that fled the country have been maintained intact in neighboring Honduras and El Salvador. The slogan "Hands Off Nicaragua!" should become the rallying cry of all those who support the right of the Nicaraguan people to determine for themselves what kind of society they want to construct.

*　　　*　　　*

The Nicaraguan workers and peasants have entered the center stage of their country's history. One of the most significant changes that they are making is the land reform.

A high percentage of the arable land in the country was owned by Somoza and his immediate circle. This land has been nationalized. Under the direction of Sandinista leader Jaime Wheelock, the Nicaraguan Institute of Agrarian Reform (INRA) has been set up. The INRA is supervising the distribution of these vast holdings to the thousands of Nicaraguan peasants who have historically eked out a subsistence on tiny plots.

In an interview reprinted in this book, Jaime Wheelock points out that

in some cases we will solve the problem of the landless peasants by giving them land. In other cases we are going to solve the problem of the landless agricultural laborers by incorporating them into production and giving them stable year-round work while providing big social and economic benefits.

And in the case of the Indian communities based on traditional systems of production, the land will be given not to the individual producer but to the whole Indian community. They will get sufficient land to increase their production and raise their standard of living.

This land reform is being enthusiastically welcomed by the peasants and farm workers, who have mobilized in large demonstrations. Peasant militias are being organized to defend the new property relations in the countryside.

For now, the Sandinistas say they are limiting the land reform to the Somocista (Somozaist) holdings. However, when reporters asked INRA director Wheelock what they will do if the lands run out and there are still needy peasants, he answered: "We'll take the rest of it."

The land reform is crucial for the Nicaraguan revolution, because 60 percent of the population lives in the country-side. Nicaragua's main export products are all agricultural—cotton, coffee, sugar, and beef.

In addition to all the Somocista property, the new government has also nationalized all of Nicaragua's banks. This gives it control over the vast bulk of the country's industrial wealth. This will be crucial for reactivating the economy, providing jobs, and meeting the needs of the workers and peasants.

Another bold step was taken on August 25 against the Somocistas, who had taken an estimated $4 billion out of the country. With the slogan, "Let's take back from Somocismo (Somozaism) the money that belongs to the people," the government declared that all 500 and 1,000 *córdoba* bills (US$50 and $100) would be immediately invalid. Everyone in the country was urged to deposit all their large denomination bills in the banks, and the borders into Nicaragua were closed for two days during the currency exchange. In return, depositors received coupons to be refunded in six months, with 8 percent interest.

Those who deposited sums no larger than 3,000 *córdobas*—60 percent of the depositors, and clearly comprised overwhelmingly of working people—were able to choose to be reimbursed or to leave their savings in the bank. Larger depositors, however, are being investigated and decisions concerning reimbursement will be made case by case.

The Ministry of Social Welfare, headed by Lea Guido de López, has announced decrees against all kinds of speculators and profiteers, decrees characterized by a deeply egalitarian spirit. The large number of buildings formerly owned by Somoza and the Somocistas will not be monopolized by private individuals or government administrators for personal use. Instead, they are to be transformed into schools, child-care centers, sports centers, museums, and cultural centers.

Government control has been established over all important exportable agricultural commodities, including cotton, coffee, sugar, and fish.

Sandinista leader Daniel Ortega has announced the refusal to pay the debts that the Somoza dictatorship accumulated in buying arms used against the people. His speech on Nicaragua's new foreign policy to the September 1979 summit conference of nonaligned nations is included in this book.

The capitalist army and police force—Somoza's National Guard—was completely routed by the popular insurrection. There is nothing left of the Guard inside the country except for scattered terrorist bands that have staged nighttime attacks on unarmed civilians and on Sandinista patrols.

But outside of these small bands, the capitalists have no armed forces within the borders of Nicaragua. The entire military apparatus has been dissolved.

The masses have been armed.

The youth of Nicaragua are being integrated into a new revolutionary army. And the people in the workers' districts and in the countryside who carried on the anti-Somoza struggle are being organized into militia units.

The Sandinista leaders are trying to move as rapidly as possible to build a strong, well-equipped, and well-trained army to meet the threat of foreign intervention and to put a stop to terrorist snipers.

In the cities—especially in the working-class and poor districts—Sandinista Defense Committees have been formed on a block-by-block basis to oversee the distribution of emergency food aid, organize the reconstruction of housing and other buildings destroyed by Somoza's bombings, and work with the Sandinista militias.

Workers in the factories, stores, banks, and other workplaces have also formed committees. These are usually elected by assemblies of all the workers. They are to form the basis of a new Sandinista Workers Federation, which will integrate the trade unions that existed under the dictatorship with the new workers' committees. It is to include the agricultural workers as well, who are being organized into the Farm Workers Association.

The government has decreed that all wages lost by workers during the June-July insurrection must be paid in full. The workers' committees are organizing to see that this is enforced.

The FSLN has helped to initiate the July 19 Sandinista Youth to organize Nicaraguan youth, who were in the front lines of the war against Somoza. The Association of Nicaraguan Women is also being formed, based on AMPRONAC, a group that mobilized women against the dictatorship.

The revolution's leaders have also announced some longer-range plans to improve the living conditions of the Nicaraguan people. Chief among these is an ambitious campaign against illiteracy modeled on the example of what was done in Cuba after the 1959 revolution there.

Some 60 percent of Nicaraguans do not know how to read and write. To remedy this situation, 1980 has been declared the "Year of Education." Brigades of teachers—many of them high school and college students—will be trained to carry out the literacy drive. They will fan out to all the cities, towns, and villages of Nicaragua to teach basic skills.

Other steps being planned include the construction of clinics and child-care centers, and the introduction of family-planning programs to make safe methods of birth control available to all women.

The five-member Junta of the Government of National Reconstruction has also instituted a far-reaching bill of rights, which is the third item in this collection. In addition to guaranteeing basic democratic rights such as freedom of speech and assembly, the Statute on the Rights of Nicaraguans outlines a broad range of economic, social, and cultural policies.

The way for all these revolutionary measures was opened by the mass upheaval that brought down the imperialist-backed Somoza dictatorship. In the course of the struggle, the Sandinista National Liberation Front came to the head of the insurgent masses.

The upsurge that brought forty-five years of Somoza tyranny to an end began in January 1978. Outraged by the assassination of opposition newspaper editor Pedro Joaquín Chamorro, the urban masses of Managua and other major cities carried out street demonstrations and a two-week general strike against Somoza.

In March 1978, uprisings against the National Guard took place in the combative Indian communities of Monimbó in Masaya and Subtiava in León. Strikes by students and workers, protest marches, and clashes with the National Guard went on constantly during subsequent months.

In August 1978, the Sandinista Front staged a spectacular raid on the National Palace in Managua. They held dozens of Somocista politicians hostage for several days and secured the release of all Sandinista prisoners— including central leader Tomás Borge—and the payment of a large sum of money.

The raid captured the imagination of the Nicaraguan people and greatly enhanced the FSLN's popularity. Thousands turned out to cheer as the victorious commando unit drove from the National Palace to the airport with its hostages.

The August raid was quickly followed by uprisings in several major cities. Civil war raged for three weeks, and only by brutally bombing the civilian population was Somoza's National Guard able to achieve a temporary victory.

As a result of the September experience, the masses became convinced that only an all-out military drive could dislodge the dictatorship.

Under the leadership of the Sandinista Front and the United People's Movement (a coalition of trade unions, working-class parties, student groups, and other organizations), committees and militia units were set up, arms were gathered, emergency food supplies were stashed away, and courses were taught in street fighting, barricade-building, and the use of weapons.

At the same time, hundreds of youth who had fled the cities after September were given military training and organized into fighting units of the FSLN.

The final offensive against the dictatorship began May 29, 1979, when Sandinista columns launched attacks on National Guard positions near the Costa Rican border.

On June 4, a general strike called by the FSLN shut down nearly all industry, transportation, and commerce in Nicaragua.

City after city fell to the rebels in subsequent weeks. The noose tightened around Somoza, who was holed up in his "bunker" in Managua, the capital.

An eyewitness to the struggles in Managua, described the events there in an interview that appeared in the August 24, 1979, issue of the socialist weekly, the *Militant:*

The insurrection in Managua really began on June 10. As always, the eastern districts of the city—the working-class districts, the areas where the poor population lives—were the ones most active in the insurrection.

Barricades were built with whatever materials available. The streets of Managua are made of paving stones, which are easily removed and used for barricades. As a matter of fact, these stones were all produced in Somoza's cement factory. They were indispensable for the building of barricades throughout the city.

The National Guard followed the same tactics it had used in September, regrouping in its central barracks, abandoning the smaller posts and entrenching itself in others. Many smaller barracks were attacked and destroyed by the insurrectionary forces in struggles that lasted one or two days.

What took place here was a popular insurrection, in the fullest political and military sense of the term. The masses participated actively; they found ways to make arms—contact bombs and molotov cocktails; they recovered small arms, .22 caliber pistols, and so on.

As the insurrection unfolded, the Guard began to concentrate its attacks, preceding them with "aerial softening" with bombs weighing 150 to 500 pounds. Some fell on inhabited areas and caused severe damage.

On June 28, the organized Sandinista forces were obliged by the Guard counterattack to retreat from Managua.

The situation partially returned to "normal," but the general strike of shopkeepers, artisans, and workers continued. The Somocista forces were incapable of even restoring basic public services.

Elsewhere in the country, the Sandinista offensive

gained momentum. After failing to gain any support from Latin American regimes for a military intervention, Washington decided to force Somoza to resign in hopes of preventing the revolutionary overthrow of the dictatorship. Somoza and many of his top generals fled to Miami on July 17. Francisco Urcuyo was named president and a new general staff was designated for the National Guard.

It was widely believed that Urcuyo would simply hand power over to the provisional government already named by the Sandinistas. But instead, Somoza's successor declared over nationwide television that he intended to stay until 1981. The *Militant* report explained what happened next in Managua:

After Urcuyo's speech, skepticism turned to popular anger. That same night you could hear the clanging of pots and pans, the sound of small demonstrations.

As word spread the next day that rebel forces were on the march toward Managua, people came into the streets without fear. I saw many demonstrations, thousands and thousands of people in the middle-class and working-class districts, even while the National Guard was still confronting the people in the streets.

Throughout the night there were bonfires, demonstrations, the clanging of pots and pans. People went right into the Guardsmen's houses and took their arms. The Guardsmen were desperate.

Desertions from the Guard numbered in the thousands, while the masses marched forward. And if the people didn't collect all the arms from the Guard in their homes, they took away the rest of them in their barracks.

Urcuyo and the remaining generals fled early in the morning on July 19, while their army was collapsing underneath them. Thousands of Managuans gathered at the "bunker" a short time later, along with an FSLN column that had just arrived from León. The eyewitness account continues:

At first, the people stopped about 200 meters from the bunker, still cautious. There were rumors that the bunker had been mined, that there were still snipers posted there, that some Guardsmen would still put up resistance. But this did not happen.

The Sandinista troops from León marched into the bunker behind a small tank. They asked the people to wait, but the people paid no attention. They went in, broke down doors, poured through the offices, the arsenals, everywhere. Some were curious, others sought arms, others came simply to be able to say "I was there." There must have been more than 10,000 persons who went into the bunker that morning.

The bunker was not just Somoza's residence; all the major military installations were located there. The people went in, the militia went in; there was euphoria, happiness. Many weapons were confiscated by the people; they found high-caliber arms, and uniforms. Their joy is difficult to put into words.

Little by little, order was restored. By two in the afternoon, other guerrilla columns were entering the city—from Masaya, from Estelí and Matagalpa, from Rivas. All hurried to be the first to enter Managua; all were cheered and applauded by the people. They began to take up positions, to take charge of the military installations, and to organize themselves.

In the course of the nineteen-month upsurge that finally brought down Somoza, the Sandinista National Liberation Front came to be the undisputed leadership of the revolution. Its bold actions against the dictator's armed forces and its determination to destroy Somocismo root and branch led the masses to view it in this way.

The FSLN is rooted in Nicaragua's long tradition of anti-imperialist struggle and plebeian radicalism. It takes its name from Augusto César Sandino, a former oilfield mechanic and mine worker who led a seven-year war of national liberation against the U.S. Marines from 1927 to 1934. When all the bourgeois-nationalist forces capitulated to the imperialists and their puppets, Sandino and his worker and peasant forces continued to fight.

The Somoza dynasty was established in 1933 with the U.S.-backed installation of Somoza Debayle's father, General Anastasio Somoza García, as the head of the National Guard. On Somoza García's orders, Sandino was assassinated in 1934, but the memory of his struggle lived on in Nicaragua. In 1962, Sandino's tradition fused with the fresh wave of radicalism that swept Nicaraguan youth after the victory of the Cuban revolution.

Founded by Carlos Fonseca Amador and other young rebels who broke with the reformism of the Stalinist Nicaraguan Socialist Party, the FSLN regrouped those who wanted to learn from the Cuban experience and end the imperialist domination of Nicaragua.

Portrait of Somoza defaced by the word *DOG*

Victorious Nicaraguans drag statue of Somoza's father through the streets of Managua.

The Sandinistas experienced many setbacks in their repeated efforts to defeat Somoza's National Guard through guerrilla warfare. Most of the original cadres lost their lives—Carlos Fonseca himself was murdered by the Guard in 1976. But when the masses began to move against Somoza in 1978, the Sandinistas were there to provide the revolutionary leadership necessary to oust the dictator.

Throughout their history, the FSLN fighters have enjoyed the active solidarity of the Cuban revolution. Now, with the revolutionary victory, Cuba is sending medical teams, teachers, and other aid to help in the reconstruction of Nicaragua.

Throughout Cuba, the workers and peasants have celebrated the victory in Nicaragua as if it were their own. As Fidel Castro put it in his speech on July 26 that is included in this book, Cubans "see ourselves mirrored in [the Nicaraguans], because nothing reminds us more of our own struggles, our sacrifices, and our own image in those early days of the revolution."

Since coming to power, the Sandinistas have continued to mobilize the workers and peasants. On August 3, for example, the FSLN called for a march and rally to dedicate a highway in Managua to the martyrs of the struggle. The march was built through the Sandinista Defense Committees.

Fifty thousand people turned out, from Managua's total population of about 600,000. The vast bulk of the marchers came in organized contingents from the poor and working-class neighborhoods, with handwritten signs in support of the revolution. They chanted slogans like "Workers and peasants to power" and "Somoza and the Yankees—they're the same thing." There was a high consciousness that this revolution belongs to the poor, to the workers and peasants.

Such consciousness is being encouraged by the FSLN. Radio Sandino and the Sandinista Television Network broadcast revolutionary songs and speeches and carry news of anti-imperialist struggles in other countries. The FSLN's daily paper, *Barricada*, serves a similar purpose. It places special emphasis on the importance of organizing the popular committees, the trade unions, the militias, and a strong army to defend the gains of the revolution.

Fidel Castro's July 26 speech hailing the revolution was broadcast on television in Nicaragua for three days in a row and became a favorite topic of discussion.

*   *   *

The immediate tasks now facing the FSLN and the entire Nicaraguan people—feeding the population, getting production under way, rebuilding the country—are enormous.

The effects of the civil war were qualitatively more devastating than what the Cubans faced in 1959 after the overthrow of Batista. Many of Nicaragua's factories were destroyed. Cities were left in ruins. Many crops were not planted because of the fighting. Nearly 2 percent of the country's population of 2.5 million people were killed.

There is hunger inside Nicaragua today. There just isn't enough food and the international aid isn't sufficient.

Alfonso Robelo, a member of the five-person Government of National Reconstruction, told the July 26 rally in Holguín, Cuba:

We have found a country destroyed. Destroyed by the bombs dropped by Somoza's air force, which bombed our cities indiscriminately. Destroyed as a result of 45 years of plunder by a corrupt regime. In fact, what we have now is a completely bankrupt country: our reserves were plundered; the people's money, down to the last cent, was spent on weapons to use against the people. . . .

Robelo also outlined the goals the government has set for itself:

We must rebuild our economy; we must provide food for our population that is presently suffering terrible shortages; we must carry out a gigantic literacy campaign so that the more than 60 percent of our people who are now illiterate will learn how to read and write; we must see to it that every Nicaraguan child has a school, no matter how humble, to begin the next school year; we need doctors to go into our countryside for the first time and provide medical care for our peasants. And for all these tasks we need the assistance of all the sister peoples of the Americas, and the people of Cuba have a special place in this process.

The masses of Nicaragua want a society of equality.

They want an end to the plunder of their resources and the exploitation of their people by U.S. corporations. They want to build a new Nicaragua in which—as in revolutionary Cuba—the needs of the workers and peasants come first, not capitalist profits. And they have shown that they are ready to do whatever is necessary to achieve these goals.

That is why Washington hates and fears the revolutionary process under way in Nicaragua. Those who have profited from the misery of the Nicaraguan people for decades know that full employment, higher living standards, land for the peasants, democratic rights for the masses, and freedom from foreign domination are all incompatible with continued capitalist rule in Nicaragua.

What the U.S. capitalists fear most is that the FSLN and the Nicaraguan workers and peasants—organized, armed, and determined—will follow the example of Cuba.

Nicaragua under Somoza was a bastion of U.S. domination over the entire region—the launching pad for the CIA-sponsored invasions of Guatemala in 1954 and Cuba in 1961. Nicaragua under the FSLN has already become an inspiration to the workers and peasants throughout Latin America, especially in neighboring El Salvador, Guatemala, and Honduras, all suffering under U.S.-backed dictatorships.

Thus, while the governments of the United States and the European capitalist countries pretend to be sympathetic to the needs and aspirations of the Nicaraguan people, they are scheming to block the revolutionary process and to roll back the gains it has made.

One side of their counterrevolutionary plan is military: maintaining Somoza's forces in Honduras, El Salvador, and Miami. It takes a lot of money to keep these troops armed and organized for any length of time, and that money can have only one source: Washington.

But overt military action by Washington against Nicaragua faces big obstacles. Working people in the United States are adamantly opposed to any new Vietnams. They don't want to be sent to fight and die to impose dictatorships subservient to Washington.

Moreover, even a camouflaged U.S. military operation would provoke a massive protest in the United States and throughout Latin America. What is even worse, from

Washington's point of view, is that such a limited military move might not succeed. It is likely that a Bay of Pigs-style invasion of Nicaragua would confront not only the armed people of Nicaragua, but the battle-hardened combat forces of revolutionary Cuba as well.

As Fidel warned on July 26, U.S. military intervention would mean "a gigantic Vietnam . . . throughout Central America and in the rest of Latin America, a gigantic Vietnam."

Before playing that last desperate card, the U.S. imperialists are first trying economic blackmail and maneuvers. The aid coming from the U.S. government—a tiny amount, grudgingly given—is intended to make it easier for Washington to demand political concessions from the Nicaraguan government.

Over 300 tons a day of food are desperately needed in Nicaragua. But after all the devastation the U.S. government has brought on Nicaragua in the past decades, Washington's aid for reconstruction so far amounts to a mere $7 million. Together with an additional $9 million approved by a congressional subcommittee on September 11, this is just a drop in the bucket.

The U.S. aid has still another purpose: to drive a wedge into the Sandinista leadership and the new government, to split them, to try to find some sectors that would, under economic pressure, begin to bend to Washington's demands and help strengthen and consolidate the capitalist forces that still exist in Nicaragua.

Here too, judging from the actions of the Sandinista leadership and the new government, the imperialists are not meeting with success. Far from drawing back, the FSLN leaders are moving forward in mobilizing and arming the masses to fight for their interests.

The imperialists are also trying to sow confusion and division among supporters of the Nicaraguan revolution. One incident that the big business press seized upon was the expulsion of the non-Nicaraguan members of the Simón Bolívar Brigade from Nicaragua in mid-August. This brigade was an armed international contingent that had been initiated by the Partido Socialista de los Trabajadores (PST—Socialist Workers Party) of Colombia in June with the ostensible purpose of militarily aiding the FSLN in the final offensive against the Somoza regime.

The Simón Bolívar Brigade promoted policies in direct opposition to the FSLN while masquerading in Sandinista uniforms and carrying Sandinista banners. They attempted to call strikes in nationalized industries and to organize unauthorized land occupations in the name of the FSLN. They opposed the formation of the revolutionary army and the turning in of arms to the FSLN. The brigade's refusal to cease functioning as an armed organization masquerading as part of the FSLN led to the expulsion of its non-Nicaraguan members.

The brigade's non-Nicaraguan members were put on a plane that stopped over in Panama, where the Torrijos regime utilized the opportunity to arrest and beat members of the brigade before sending them on. The FSLN leadership then issued a statement explaining that its intention was solely to expel them from Nicaragua.

Because the Colombian PST, which initiated the brigade, is a sympathizing organization of the Fourth International, the worldwide Trotskyist organization, the imperialist press falsely labeled the brigade as "Trotskyist." But the actions of the brigade were in direct opposition to the policies of the Fourth International, which is carrying out an international campaign in solidarity with the Nicaraguan revolution in collaboration with the FSLN and not in opposition to it.

The article "Imperialism Launches Propaganda Drive Against Sandinistas," by Barry Sheppard and Mary-Alice Waters, two leaders of the Socialist Workers Party of the U.S., analyzes how the big business press attempted to utilize the Simón Bolívar Brigade expulsion to attack the Nicaraguan revolution. It is included as an appendix to this collection.

*   *   *

The power that exists today in Nicaragua is a revolutionary power. A government independent of the old ruling classes has been established, which is mobilizing the power of the workers and their allies to implement progressive social measures that more and more challenge the economic prerogatives of capital.

While capitalism has been dealt a stunning blow, it still

exists. The capitalists and those determined to defend their interests still remain a factor in Nicaragua. Nevertheless, the direction in which the Sandinista leadership is moving is toward deepening the revolutionary mobilization of the masses to defend their interests.

The Sandinistas have proven themselves to be a revolutionary leadership in overthrowing the Somoza dictatorship and destroying the old armed forces of the capitalists. And they are proving themselves in action after taking power, by mobilizing and arming the masses to defend their own interests.

The working class of the entire world will see the Nicaraguan revolution as its own. Nicaragua will gain enormous solidarity from the workers of other countries, including the United States.

Revolutionary Cuba has set the example by its self-sacrificing support and by calling on all countries to compete in sending reconstruction aid to Nicaragua. Their dedication to the Nicaraguan cause can help inspire a wave of solidarity throughout the Americas.

Around the world, the Fourth International has campaigned to get out the truth about the Nicaraguan revolution. In a statement issued on August 15, 1979, the United Secretariat of the Fourth International urged the launching of a broad solidarity campaign:

> The Fourth International calls on the mass parties and organizations of the workers movement to build the broadest possible international movement—united and nonexclusionary—in support of the struggle of the Nicaraguan people and the fighters of the FSLN, whose courage has become a most precious heritage of the world proletariat.
> Immediate aid to Nicaragua!
> Imperialist hands off!
> No threats against Cuba!
> Solidarity with the Nicaraguan Revolution!

The Sandinistas too have a slogan, a quote from Sandino, whose meaning they feel very deeply. They say:

"The sons of Sandino neither sell out nor give up. They will be free or dead."

That is the commitment they are making inside Nicaragua. They are organizing and educating the workers and peasants, the entire young generation, to prepare to give their lives to free Nicaragua and through that to help the Latin American and world revolution. With the aid and solidarity of working people throughout the world, they can be successful.

Pedro Camejo and Fred Murphy
Managua, Nicaragua
September 25, 1979

Fred Halstead

Nicaraguan tenant farmers from the province of Granada

Nicaragua's Plans for Agriculture: Interview with Jaime Wheelock

Question. Could you begin by describing the situation in agriculture in recent years under the dictatorship?

Answer. We have two basic types of production. One is cereals for the domestic market; the other is production for export.

Most production for export was carried out under conditions that left agricultural workers idle a large part of the year. Export production was mainly aimed at fulfilling the needs of a very small layer of owners who held large tracts of land.

Two families—the Somozas and the Pellas—controlled more than 500,000 acres of cotton, about 250,000 acres of coffee, 200,000 head of cattle, somewhat more than 35,000 acres of sugar cane. Large holdings in tobacco and rice were basically controlled by the Somocistas.

Along with the division between production for export and production for internal consumption, there is also a division between a highly capitalist sector of agriculture and a sector we could call poor and medium peasants.

In fact, between 40 and 60 percent of the arable land was controlled by the Somoza family. And the figure rises to about 70 percent if we add the holdings of the Somocistas.

The remaining land is controlled by about 60,000 peasants who have very small holdings, and some 100,000 peasants who do a combination of paid labor and labor on their own small plots. Many workers, even middle peasants with family farms, had to work during the planting or harvesting seasons on the large farms.

In the case of the cotton-growing industry alone, more than 250,000 agricultural workers are employed at the height of the picking. The coffee industry needs 150,000 workers during the height of the season.

In the case of sugar, some 15,000 workers are employed at the high point.

All this means that there is a proletarian mass in agriculture, but it is a seasonal proletariat, a fluid proletariat—sometimes working in cotton, then in coffee, then in sugar.

In short, the capitalist export sector, as well as the wasteful agricultural oligarchy, combined to displace the small producers, the small peasants.

In Chinandega, for example, almost all the land is covered by sugar, cotton, and banana plantations; the peasant masses have been driven from their land.

The peasants lead miserable lives in the countryside; the phenomenon of marginal neighborhoods that have arisen in the cities, is also taking place in the countryside. It is incredible. You find people living miserable lives in the countryside, suffocating on the land.

A separate development has taken place in which peasants who have lost their land have moved to the outskirts of the cities, where they live in shantytowns. You also have the case of some peasants, like those in the Chinandega area, who have almost been driven into the sea, where they eke out a living through fishing.

Q. What measures are being taken to resolve this problem?

A. In the northern part of the country, where there are no roads, no infrastructure, and land that is not very productive, we want to carry out a program of enlarging the landholdings of the peasants, combined with technical and development assistance.

On the other hand, in the center of the country—in the Managua valley, in Masaya and Carazo—where we have strong one-crop production, we want to solve the land problem by giving the land to the peasants.

But in other parts of the country, for example in León, in Chinandega, and in Rivas, we do not plan to turn the land over to the peasants. There we are going to set up big state farms, which will at the same time be the basis for the economic and social development of the area.

So, in some cases we will solve the problem of the landless peasants by giving them land. In other cases we are going to solve the problem of the landless agricultural laborers by incorporating them into production and giving them stable year-round work while providing big social and economic benefits.

And in the case of the Indian communities based on traditional systems of production, the land will be given not to the individual producer but to the whole Indian community. They will get sufficient land to increase their production and raise their standard of living.

Q. What type of administration is planned for the big state farms?

A. The workers on these farms will participate in the management and help make the major decisions.

But a large portion of the production of each farm will also go toward social development—health, education, housing, and so forth—for these workers and for the whole region as well.

Take, for example, the case of Rivas, where we have a large sugar mill called Dolores. Part of the production from this mill will probably be used to help solve the problem of the lack of hospitals in the entire province.

This is the consciousness that we hope to instill in the workers. They will know that their production helped to build hospitals for the whole department, as well as to provide homes, educational programs, and literacy programs. The aim is to incorporate the workers socially, as producers, in decision-making both in the plant and in the entire society.

Q. Several days ago there was an article in 'Barricada' that reported that some peasants, I believe in León, were demanding arms to defend their gains. Will you be encouraging the development of peasant militias?

A. Yes. In fact, *there already are* peasant militias. They were built during the war, and within our army there is a high percentage of peasants. So this is not something we still have to develop.

Q. Could you explain what role the peasants played in the struggle against Somoza and in the insurrection?

A. For many years the peasants have participated directly in the struggle for democracy and freedom, for progress in Nicaragua.

This has been going on since the days of General Sandino. The peasants were the most important numerical force in that struggle for national liberation. But in this new stage as well, the first nuclei of the Sandinista Front grew in the mountains with the support of the peasants. The peasants here have been the social layer that has been hit hardest by the blows of the repression.

It is enough to recall a single example, although there are many. Somoza launched a wave of brutal repression against the peasants in the north in 1975-76 and 1977. Towns like Barial, Sofana, Boca de Lulu were totally leveled. Barial ceased to exist.

The Somocista gangs killed thousands of peasants. But despite all that, the peasants have always been involved in combative and patriotic activity. For that reason we have a great debt of honor to the peasants. Moreover, the peasantry is the motor force of this revolution, and it is the first beneficiary of this revolution.

Q. Finally, what can workers in the United States do to help defend the Nicaraguan revolution?

A. First I want to use the *Militant* to salute the people in the United States who have understood and been in solidarity with our struggle. Moreover, we have received medical, financial, and material aid from the American people.

At the same time that they were aiding us, they were protesting the aid given to Somoza.

This has given us a great deal of optimism about the consciousness that exists among the American people regarding the right of other peoples to their self-determination.

It has also given us confidence that the American people will actively participate in defending those rights and in giving solidarity and aid to those who are struggling for just causes.

We are optimistic regarding the future of the struggle in the United States, and in the heightening of the consciousness of the American people and the American workers.

Today there is one big job, one immediate task, and that is to prevent and actively oppose the plans for political aggression that are being cooked up by recalcitrant, reactionary sectors in the United States.

It is important to maintain this consciousness of the American people in order to oppose any aggressive plans.

In addition, we need economic aid to rebuild the country. The United States told us that it was going to send 300, 400 tons of aid daily. So far only one plane has arrived. That's all.

They are playing around with the aid, perhaps to put pressure on us. But the fact is that the aid has not gotten here, although the American people are in favor of giving it to the people of Nicaragua.

You have seen what it is like here. There is no food, there are no seeds to plant, there is no money. The Somocistas left us a state in ruins, and now they are trying to paralyze international solidarity.

So in the first place we need immediate aid—food, clothing, medicine, help in reconstruction.

And in addition, we need pressure to grant loans to Nicaragua, long-term low-interest loans so that we can rebuild our country.

"My cause is the cause of my people, the cause of America, the cause of all the oppressed peoples."

Portrait of Sandino hangs at an August 28, 1979, rally in Managua.

Nothing Will Hold Back
Our Struggle for Liberation

by Daniel Ortega

In January 1928 the Panamerican Conference was held in Havana. At that time the Nicaraguan people were engaged in an unequal struggle against Yankee intervention. Calvin Coolidge, who was then president of the United States, participated in the Havana meeting, and the tyrant Machado was president of Cuba.

Sandino, hoping to gain the support of some delegations, sent the following message on January 2, 1928:

Our voices must be heard in Havana. Men must not lack the moral courage to speak the truth about our misfortune. They must tell how the people of Nicaragua, who are valiantly fighting and suffering, are determined to make any sacrifice, even including their own extermination, in order to defend their liberty. The results in Havana will be null and void if the ideal of the Spanish-speaking peoples is not crystallized; if you let us be assassinated to the last man, we will have the consolation of knowing that we carried out our duty. Our Country and Freedom.

A. C. Sandino

Not a single voice was raised at that Havana meeting.

Today Havana is serving as the site for this Sixth Summit, and the peoples and governments that are represented in this assembly are motivated by common interests.

A free and hospitable people, filled with solidarity, is receiving these delegations. And the leader of the revolution carried out by this people is presiding over the

Nonaligned for this period. The tyrant Machado no longer governs Cuba. It is the people of Cuba who determine their own destiny.

The Government of National Reconstruction of Nicaragua and the Sandinista National Liberation Front salute the people of Cuba, their government, and the president of the Council of State, Comandante and Comrade Fidel Castro.

We also salute the peoples of Latin America, the Caribbean, Africa, and Asia for the solidarity they demonstrated in support of our cause.

On Saturday, September 1, in a Mexican newspaper, we read a dispatch datelined Havana that made reference to Nicaragua's position regarding the "problem" of Kampuchea. And we say "problem" because it is a problem for imperialism for *a people to be free.*

The dispatch in question noted that Nicaragua's delegation had aligned itself with the Soviet bloc by recognizing the Government of People's Kampuchea. We all know what interests motivate the international press agencies of the so-called free world, so the deed does not surprise us.

We know that many of these press agencies, and with them the most reactionary sectors of the United States government and of Latin America, are waiting to pounce on our declarations at this meeting.

These are the same forces that gave rise to the Somocista dictatorship. They are the same forces that defamed and assassinated Lumumba, that defamed and assassinated Che. These are the same forces that slandered and assassinated [Vietnamese freedom fighter] Van Troi, the same forces that slandered and assassinated Sandino.

Imperialism cannot conceive of a free people, a sovereign people, an independent people. Because, simply and plainly, for them *the people* is nothing more than an empty phrase. We just saw reconfirmation of this when our final offensive was launched.

They examined the war in mathematical terms. Somoza had a regular army. Somoza had more soldiers than the Sandinistas. Somoza had tanks, planes, artillery, while the Sandinistas didn't. Somoza had more soldiers, more rifles, more communications than the Sandinistas. Therefore, Somoza had to win the war against the Sandinistas. But what was left out was that Somoza did not have the people, and that we Sandinistas were the people.

And when Somoza was losing the war, they were talking about Costa Rican intervention, Panamanian intervention, Cuban intervention, Soviet intervention—simply because they have never been able to understand, and are never going to understand, that people are capable of achieving their liberation, that people are able to solidarize themselves with people, and that therefore the free and sovereign people of Nicaragua today recognizes the right of Kampuchea to occupy this seat.

I repeat, imperialism cannot understand it because for them *the people* is nothing more than an empty phrase.

The Nicaraguan people has won, with its blood, the right to be here today, in this way breaking with a historic past of servility toward imperialist policy.

For the first time in its entire history the Nicaraguan people can officially express its sovereign will, joining this movement of the Nonaligned barely forty-one days after its triumph.

We are entering the Nonaligned movement because in this movement we see the broadest organization of the Third World states that are playing an important role and exercise a growing influence in the international sphere, in the struggle of peoples against imperialism, colonialism, neocolonialism, apartheid, racism, including Zionism and every form of oppression. Because they are for active peaceful coexistence, against the existence of military blocs and alliances, for restructuring international relations on an honorable basis, and are for the establishment of a new international economic order.

In the Sandinista revolution there is no alignment; there is an absolute and consistent commitment to the aspirations of the peoples who have achieved their independence and to those who are struggling to win it. That is why we are among the Nonaligned.

This transcendental step is part of the process of liberation that peoples are going through, peoples such as those in Grenada, Iran, Kampuchea, and Uganda, who won beautiful victories this year.

In 1855 a certain William Walker arrived from the southern slave states of the United States with a gang of mercenaries, to make himself master of our country and of all of Central America.

The individual in question named himself president of Nicaragua and his first decree was the reestablishment of slavery; the United States press and more than a few U.S. legislators made William Walker into a hero.

In September 1856, after continual and bloody resistance, the people of Nicaragua and the peoples of Central America defeated the invader, who was obliged to flee to his country of origin, where he was received as a hero.

Some months later he again tried to invade our country. During his third attempt he was captured in Honduras, a country bordering on Nicaragua, and was shot. In 1909 a liberal president named José Santos Zelaya, who tried to open new markets in Europe, was forced to resign by a note sent by the U.S. secretary of state of that time. But what Señor Zelaya lacked, the Nicaraguan people had plenty of, and they then rose up against Yankee intervention.

Because we reject Yankee intervention we are in the Nonaligned. For that reason, and because we are Sandinistas, we demand the reintegration, the unconditional return of the Guantánamo base to Cuba, and we recognize the heroic and unequal struggle waged by the Cuban people against the criminal blockade.

That is why we support the struggle of the people of Puerto Rico for self-determination and independence, and why we are in solidarity with Lolita Lebrón and her companions in prison, who are authentic representatives of the struggle of the people of Puerto Rico.

That is why we stand behind the people of Panama in their struggle for sovereignty over the Canal Zone.

That is why we are with the people of Belize in their struggle for independence, for self-determination, and for territorial integrity.

Regular troops of the Yankee marines landed in our country in 1910 in an attempt to suppress our people's desire for independence. Bloody struggles were unleashed and this armed intervention was maintained until 1926, the year they withdrew, believing the situation to be under control.

Because we are Sandinistas and because just causes are

our causes, we have, from the beginning, identified with the struggle of the heroic people of Vietnam, and we condemn all the aggressions that have taken place and are taking place against the people and government of Vietnam, which fought, and is fighting, against aggression and foreign occupation.

We also support the just struggle of the people of Western Sahara, and from this moment Nicaragua must be included among the countries that fully recognize the Democratic Arab Sahraoui Republic and the POLISARIO Front as the only and the legitimate representative of the heroic people of Western Sahara.

That is why we recognize the legitimate rights of the people of Namibia, represented by SWAPO. We support the Patriotic Front of Zimbabwe, the sole representative of this people, and we condemn the imperialist maneuvers in Rhodesia, the puppet regime of Muzorewa, and the so-called internal settlement.

We solidarize ourselves with the frontline countries and condemn the aggression by South Africa and Rhodesia against them. And we solidarize with the right of the people of East Timor to self-determination.

We support the reunification of Korea and we demand the withdrawal of U.S. troops from South Korea.

Only a few months were to pass when in 1927 Yankee marines again landed on our soil.

Then the figure of Augusto César Sandino vigorously rose up and, at the head of an army of workers and peasants, sought to militarily defeat the interventionist forces in an unequal campaign.

Sandino embodied the desire for liberty of a people who were systematically subjected to the attack of Yankee intervention and subjected to imperialist exploitation and domination. The same marines who had murdered the Filipino people thousands of miles from our country, arrived to soak Nicaraguan territory in blood in those days.

This explains the existence of Sandinismo, which on May 4, 1927, gave rise to what Sandino called the "war of liberators to end the war of the oppressors."

The Yankees, who were unable to defeat Sandino's army militarily, who found themselves forced to withdraw in

January 1932, again resorted to treachery, using as their instrument an army and an army chief named Anastasio Somoza García, founder of the dynasty. This army and this army chief were created by the White House strategists to assassinate Sandino.

They thought that killing Sandino would solve the problem. They did not take into account that Sandino had initiated a process of liberation which, carried on by the Sandinista National Liberation Front, was to win one of its most important victories on July 19, 1979. On that day we both defeated the criminal Somocista National Guard and expelled the last Yankee marine, Anastasio Somoza, from Nicaragua.

Our country is a small country, a poor country.

A little more than 2.5 million Nicaraguans live in 128,000 square kilometers. It is a country that is basically dependent on agriculture, and its production was paralyzed by the war. A country that had few factories, which were destroyed by the Somoza air force.

A country with a small population that has had to sacrifice thousands of its best children to repel three armed Yankee interventions that have left more than 200,000 victims. A country that in its final offensive against the Somocista dictatorship suffered more than 50,000 deaths, a high percentage of whom, 90 percent of the total, were youth from eight years of age to twenty.

A country with its schools and hospitals destroyed, with its cities leveled by 500-pound bombs given to Somoza by the United States and Israeli Zionism. But we were not alone in the struggle. We know that we had the backing of the peoples of the world. We know that this was what made it impossible for the Yankees to carry out a new armed intervention in our country before the tyrant was destroyed.

Among the files abandoned by Somocismo we have found proof of the loans for arms that the government of Israel had given to the dictatorship. Israel was an accomplice to the crimes of Somoza. Israel was the instrument that imperialism used up to the last moment to arm Somoza's genocidal dictatorship. Rockets, rifles, howitzers, planes, gunboats, and even helmets and uniforms were sent to the dictator. But the strength of the people was greater than that of the aggression.

As we said at that time, we will not repay these loans, this debt that adds up to millions of dollars. Nor will we pay any debt contracted with other countries for armaments for the Somocista regime. On the contrary, it is Israel that owes a debt to our people.

We are Sandinistas; our people have been struggling against oppression and interventions for more than 150 years. That is why we have historically identified with the struggle of the Palestinian people and we recognize the PLO as their legitimate representative. And that is why we condemn Israeli occupation of the Arab territories and demand their unconditional return.

We support genuine efforts in the search for a just and true peace in the Middle East. But such a peace must take into account the interests of all the parties, and in the first place the rights of the Palestinian people.

On May 4, 1927, at the moment Sandino was rising up, a Nicaraguan traitor signed away the sovereignty of the people of Nicaragua to the Yankee government, in exchange for a dollar for each rifle turned in. We condemn the Camp David accords, which, like the shameful treason of 1927 in Nicaragua, merit our energetic repudiation.

In June 1979, there were forces in the U.S. government that wanted to propose an invasion of our soil to the seventeenth meeting of representatives of the Organization of American States. But there were also seventeen Latin American countries that said no to the imperialist proposal.

Here we must make special mention and take recognition of the Andean Pact countries.

We should mention the names of President Rodrigo Carazo of Costa Rica; ex-President Carlos Andrés Pérez of Venezuela; President José López Portillo of Mexico; General Omar Torrijos of Panama; and Fidel Castro of Cuba—all of whom were and continue to be in solidarity with our struggle, despite the risks that such solidarity implies.

We should make special mention of the militant solidarity that Latin American fighters gave our struggle. The blood of these fighters was shed along the road to victory. We can state that Latin America helped to make this victory possible.

We are a small country that has waged war in order to win peace. And we support the establishment of a just and lasting peace that extends to all countries and regions.

We recognize the right of peoples to win their freedom through the path that is best for them, whether armed or not.

We are a poor country that wants to take the efforts and resources now being invested in defense of the revolution and invest it in tractors and plows. And we support general and complete disarmament, under strict international control. We are for an end to the arms race and we salute the SALT II accords as an important step in this direction. We demand respect for the territorial integrity of states and renunciation of the use of force in international relations. We condemn the existence of military bases.

Sandinismo is the incarnation of the nation. The Sandinista National Liberation Front, as the genuine vanguard of the great people's insurrection that defeated the dictatorship, is now pushing forward a process of national reconstruction whose first measures have been the massive expropriation of the property of Somoza and his civilian and military accomplices. So far more than 500,000 hectares, close to 50 percent of the entire arable area of the country, has been recovered by the people.

More than 180 industrial and commercial enterprises have passed into the hands of the people.

More than 400 mansions and homes have been expropriated in the interests of the people.

The banks have been nationalized.

We have begun to put an Integral Agrarian Reform Plan into effect.

Agricultural exports have been nationalized.

The exploitation of natural resources has been nationalized.

By eliminating the 500 and 1,000 *córdoba* bills [US$50 and $100] and retiring them from circulation, we are hindering the maneuvers of the defeated Somocistas to destabilize our country financially.

A real social thrust is being given to education, health, and housing.

A foreign policy of relations with all countries of the world has been established.

We have become part of the movement of the Nonaligned.

Sandinista Defense Committees have been organized as bodies of people's participation.

The Sandinista People's Army has been set up to fulfill the pressing need to guarantee the defense and advance of the revolution.

And this revolution has been expansive and generous toward its enemies. Thousands of captured soldiers have had their lives protected. Groups such as the International Red Cross were authorized to set up centers of refuge to give shelter to the Somocista criminals who were fleeing.

The revolution is marching forward. The difficulties are great. The counterrevolution is a potential threat.

There are some who assert that we are assassinating the prisoners.

There are some who are trying to put conditions on international aid. The conspiracy is powerful and the most reactionary sectors of the U.S. government have already succeeded in stopping a small grant of $8 million that the U.S. government was going to give our country.

The most reactionary sectors of the Central American region are observing our process with trepidation. We have detected concentrations of Somocista soldiers in neighboring countries. But just as we have been generous in victory, we will be inflexible in defense of the revolution.

To what has already been described, we must add the economic legacy of imperialist domination and the Somocista war of aggression.

We find ourselves with a foreign debt of more than $1.53 billion. Of this amount, $596 million falls due this year, having been incurred as short-term loans at very high interest rates. The foreign debt is equivalent to three times the total annual exports of the country.

The loans obtained by Somocismo were misspent, squandered, and sent out of the country to personal accounts in the United States and Europe.

A study published August 14 by the Economic Commission for Latin America (CEPAL) maintained that Somocista bombing resulted in $580 million in material damage to the physical and social infrastructure in the agricultural, industrial, and commercial sectors. At present $741 million is needed to reactivate production.

To the losses cited above, we have to add the losses to the

system of production that stem from the paralysis of economic activities. In addition we must add the resources required for restoring the country's economic apparatus at a time when it is also being transformed.

To give us a more graphic representation of the problem, CEPAL estimates that the situation we have described means that the Gross Domestic Product has declined 25 percent this year, 1979. In per capita terms, this puts the GDP back to the level that Nicaragua was at in 1962, meaning we have slid back seventeen years.

And to top it all off, our revolution found only $3.5 million in the state coffers. That is all that Somocismo was unable to loot.

Nicaragua's situation has provoked interest in the countries of Latin America and the rest of the world. Regional bodies have expressed their decision to aid us. Bilaterally we have close relations with many countries.

But we want to be frank: The oppressive financial problem that confronts our process, which is directly related to restructuring the foreign debt and receiving financing in order to allow our economy to start up again, does not seem to seriously interest the developed countries.

The government of Mexico, which has aided us to the extent it is able, has raised the idea of an international sale of solidarity bonds that would come due at a deferred period and with low interest. Through this bond issue the debt that falls due this year, which as we said totals $596 million, would be restructured on adequate terms. We support the proposal of President Didier Rasiratekat of Madagascar, regarding the creation of a Financial Fund of the Nonaligned Countries.

We believe it is our duty to present before the movement of the Nonaligned both the advances and the problems of the revolution in Nicaragua.

We believe that by consolidating the Nicaraguan revolution we will be strengthening the struggle of the underdeveloped countries.

We know that imperialism is interested in seeing our process fail and that it is going to use all the resources at its disposal to achieve that.

The liberation struggle in our country is continuing. And today more than ever we need the disinterested support of the Nonaligned. Nicaragua, which forty-one days after its triumph is showing you both the open wounds and the consolidation of our revolution, is a challenge for this movement.

The people of Sandino are not going to step back from the ground already gained. Our integration with the peoples of Africa and Asia raises our morale in this great battle. The future belongs to the peoples.

The march toward victory will not be stopped!

Section of the Santa Rosa barrio in Managua destroyed by bombing

Bombed out area of the Ingenio San Antonio, the largest sugar mill in Central America

Workers repair the site of a Managua barricade.

Statute on the Rights of Nicaraguans

The Junta of the Government of National Reconstruction of the Republic of Nicaragua, considering:

1. That the Somoza dictatorship's systematic disregard for the fundamental rights of the Nicaraguan people and for individual human rights led to acts of barbarism which outraged the conscience of humanity; and

2. That the basis for freedom, justice, and peace lies in the recognition and affirmation of fundamental human rights, both individual and collective, for which it is essential that these rights be protected by the revolutionary government;

Therefore in accordance with its vested authority decrees the following *Statute on the Rights of Nicaraguans.*

Title I: Rights of the People

1. The Nicaraguan people has the right to free and full choice in determining its political status and providing for its own economic, social, and cultural development.

The state shall guarantee by law the direct participation of the people in the basic affairs of the country, on both a national and a local level.

2. To accomplish its goals, the Nicaraguan people has the right to freely dispose of its natural wealth and resources, without prejudicing those obligations incurred by international cooperation based on the principle of mutual benefit, solidarity, and international justice. In no case may the Nicaraguan people be deprived of its own means of subsistence.

Title II: Individual Civil and Political Rights

3. All persons are equal before the law, and have the right to equal protection. There shall be no discrimination on the basis of birth, race, color, sex, language, religion, opinions, origin, economic position, or any other social condition.

It is the duty of the state to use all the means at its disposal to remove any obstacles which impede real equality of citizens and their participation in the political, economic, and social life of the country.

4. The state shall respect and guarantee the right recognized in this Title to all persons who are within its territory and subject to its jurisdiction. Foreigners shall not be able to intervene in the political affairs of the country.

5. The right to life is inviolable, and inherent in the human person. In Nicaragua there is no death penalty.

6. All persons have the right to respect for their physical, psychological, and moral integrity. Penalties shall not be imposed on anyone except the delinquent person.

No one shall be subjected to torture, nor to punishments or treatment which are cruel, inhuman, or degrading. It shall not be permitted to establish a punishment or punishments which, individually or together, last more than thirty years.

7. No one shall be subjected to servitude, nor constrained to carry out forced or obligatory labor. The law shall regulate obligatory labor and services that may be demanded by virtue of judicial decision. These include conditional freedom, military or civilian service, service imposed in cases of danger or disasters which threaten the lives or well-being of the community, as well as labor or service that is part of normal civic obligation.

8. Every individual has the right to personal freedom and personal security. No one may be subjected to arbitrary arrest or imprisonment, nor deprived of their freedom, except for legally established cause and in conformity with a legal proceeding. Consequently:

(1) Arrests may be carried out only under a written warrant from a competent judge or from the authorities expressly authorized by law, except in cases of *flagrante delicto.*

(2) All persons arrested shall have the right:

(*a*) To be informed and notified promptly of the reason for their arrest and of the accusation, denunciation, or charges against them;

(*b*) To be brought before the competent authority within twenty-four hours, or else set free;

(*c*) To submit a writ of *habeas corpus;*

(*d*) To be treated with the respect worthy of the inherent dignity of a human being;

(*e*) To obtain reparations in case of illegal arrest or imprisonment.

9. Persons awaiting trial shall be separated from convicted prisoners, and women from men, each receiving adequate treatment for their circumstances. Children may only be brought before Courts for Minors, and in no case shall be sent to common prisons. There shall be adaptation centers for them, under the auspices of the Ministry of Social Welfare.

10. The essential objective of the prison system shall be the reform and social rehabilitation of the convicts, seeking to incorporate them into the productive process.

11. All accused persons shall have the right, on an equal basis, to the following minimum guarantees:

(*a*) Not to be presumed guilty unless and until a formal sentence has been handed down against them;

(*b*) To be tried without delay by a competent tribunal. The judicial process must be public, although in some exceptional cases the press and the general public may be excluded from all or part of a trial for reasons of morality, public order, or national security;

(*c*) To be guaranteed the right to participate in the trial from the beginning;

(*d*) To be given the opportunity to really and effectively intervene in the proceedings, and to have adequate time and means to prepare their defense. If the defendant in his or her opening statement does not designate a defense counsel and is not an attorney, an official defense counsel shall be named immediately;

(*e*) To have a defense counsel named in cases where no counsel could be found after a public request was made;

(*f*) To intervene in the presentation and examination of all types of evidence before any verdict is handed down;

(*g*) Not to be forced to testify against himself or herself, nor to confess guilt;

(*h*) Not to have a prison sentence handed down against him or her unless all elements of the crime have been fully proven and a grave presumption of guilt exists; and to have the prison sentence handed down within ten days after the warrant for arrest;

(*i*) All persons found guilty of crimes have the right to appeal the verdict and sentence imposed on them to a higher court, as prescribed by law;

(*j*) Not to be tried again for a crime for which one has already been convicted or acquitted;

(*k*) Not to be removed from the judge having jurisdiction.

12. No one shall be convicted for acts or omissions that were not crimes under national or international law at the time they were committed. Nor shall any punishment be imposed which is more serious than the one applicable at the time of commission of the crime. If subsequent revisions of the law provide for the imposition of a lighter punishment than the one in effect at the time the crime was committed, the accused shall benefit from that revision.

None of the provisions of this article shall be construed as opposing the trial or conviction of a person for acts or omissions which at the time of commission were considered crimes according to the general principles of law recognized by the international community.

13. Trial by jury shall be provided for crimes specified by the law.

14. No one shall be imprisoned solely for the fact of being unable to fulfill an economic obligation, no matter how it may have been incurred.

15. All persons who are in Nicaraguan territory legally shall have the right to move about freely, and to freely choose their place of residence. Nicaraguans shall have the right to enter and leave the country freely.

16. The right to asylum in Nicaragua is guaranteed to any person being persecuted for fighting for the cause of

peace and justice, or for the recognition or extension of the human, civil, political, social, economic, and cultural rights of individuals or groups. If for any reason it is decided to expel an exile, he or she may never be sent to a country where he or she might be persecuted.

Extradition shall be regulated by the law and international treaties, and shall never be carried out in cases of political crimes or common crimes linked to political acts as determined by Nicaraguan standards. For the purposes of extradition, genocide shall not be considered a political crime.

17. Every human being has the right in Nicaragua to recognition of his or her judicial personality and capacity.

No person shall be obliged to do anything not required by law, nor prevented from doing anything not prohibited by law. Consequently, only on the basis of the law may personal or familial debts be imposed, except for the duties of conduct and abstention required by human solidarity, the duty to behave in a fraternal manner, respect for the rights and freedoms of others, and the need to satisfy the just demands of morality, public order, and general well-being in a democratic society, even when such duties are not expressly established by law.

18. No person shall be subjected to arbitrary or illegal interference in their private life, their family, their place of residence, their correspondence or communication, nor to attacks on their honor and reputation; all shall have the right to protection by the law in the case of such interference or attacks. In particular:

(1) A person's residence and all other private quarters are inviolable, and may only be searched on the written order of a competent judge, or to prevent the commission or concealment of crimes, or to avoid harm to persons or goods, subject to provisions of the law.

(2) Private documents and communications are inviolable. The law shall establish cases and procedures for the examination or confiscation of private documents, financial books, and related documents when it is indispensable to do so in order to clarify matters brought before courts of justice, or for fiscal purposes.

19. No one may be subjected to coercive measures that might impair their freedom of thought, conscience, and

religion, nor their right to have or to adopt the religion or beliefs of their choice, nor their freedom to manifest those beliefs individually or collectively, in public or in private, through worship, celebration of rites, practice, or preaching.

20. Freedom of information is one of the fundamental principles of authentic democracy. Therefore, it cannot be subjugated, directly or indirectly, to the economic power of any group.

21. All persons have the right to freedom of expression; this right encompasses the freedom to seek, receive, and distribute information and ideas, whether orally, or in writing, in printed or artistic form, or by any other means chosen. The exercise of these freedoms brings with it duties and responsibilities, and consequently may be subject to certain necessary formalities, conditions, and restrictions specified by law:

(*a*) In the interest of national security and integrity, public safety, and the national economy;

(*b*) For the preservation of order and prevention of crime;

(*c*) For the protection of the health, moral well-being, or the dignity of persons and the reputations or the rights of others;

(*d*) To prevent the release of confidential information or to guarantee the authority and impartiality of the Judicial Power.

22. Any propaganda against peace, and any apology for national, racial, or religious intolerance, is prohibited.

23. The right of peaceful assembly is recognized. The right to demonstrate publicly shall be regulated by police ordinances.

24. All persons have the right to freely associate with others for legal purposes.

25. All citizens shall enjoy without restriction the following rights:

(*a*) To organize political parties or groups, or to belong to them;

(*b*) To participate in the direction of public affairs, directly or through freely elected representatives;

(*c*) To petition in writing, individually or collectively, to any public functionary, official entity, or public power, and the right to obtain prompt resolution of such matters;

(*d*) To vote and to be elected, and to have generally equal access to public office.

26. All persons have the right to citizenship. No one shall be arbitrarily deprived of their citizenship, or of the right to change it.

27. Property, whether individual or collective, fulfills a social function. It may therefore be subject to restrictions in regard to ownership, benefit, use, and disposition, for reasons of security, public interest or utility, social interest, the national economy, national emergency or disaster, or for purposes of agrarian reform.

Title III: Individual Economic, Social, and Cultural Rights

Section I: Economic Rights

28. The law, taking into account as necessary the rights involved and the national economy, shall determine to what extent the economic rights recognized in this statute shall be guaranteed to persons who are not Nicaraguans.

29. Work is a right and a social responsibility of the individual. It is the duty of the state to obtain full and productive employment for all Nicaraguans under conditions which guarantee the fundamental rights of the individual.

30. All persons have the right to enjoy equitable and satisfactory conditions of work, which should assure them, in particular:

(1) Remuneration which provides the worker with at least:

(*a*) A salary or wage equal to that paid for equal work under the same conditions of efficiency, and adequate to the social responsibilities of the worker, without discrimination for reasons of sex;

(*b*) Decent conditions of existence both for the worker and for his or her family.

(2) Health and safety on the job.

(3) Equal opportunity for all to be promoted to the

appropriate job classification, with no limitations other than time of service and capability.

(4) Rest, the enjoyment of free time, reasonable limitation of the hours of work, and periodic paid vacations that provide effective rest, as well as pay for holidays.

Nothing in this article shall be construed as authorizing employers to deny workers rights or guarantees they had previously obtained, on the pretext that they are not mentioned or are mentioned less prominently in this article.

Section II: Social Rights

31. With the aim of promoting and protecting the economic and social interests of Nicaraguans, the following are guaranteed:

(1) The right to establish and promote popular, communal, neighborhood, rural, and other organizations, as well as labor or professional associations.

(2) The right to establish trade unions and to join them, subject only to the statutes of the unions themselves.

(3) The right of unions to form national federations or confederations, and the right of these to establish or affiliate to international trade union organizations.

(4) The right to establish and promote labor and production cooperatives.

32. The right to strike is recognized for all workers; it is to be exercised in conformity with the laws.

33. Every person has the right to social security; to gain satisfaction of the indispensable rights to dignity and to the full development of one's personality; to an adequate standard of living for oneself and one's family, which assures health, well-being—in particular food, clothing, shelter, medical assistance, and necessary social services; as well as social benefits in the event of unemployment, illness, maternity, physical handicap, loss of one's spouse, old age, death, orphanhood, occupational injury, or other cases of loss of one's means of subsistence.

34. The family is the natural unit of society and has the right to protection by the society and the state.

Marriage is based on the voluntary agreement of the woman and the man. In family relations there exists absolute equality of rights and responsibilities between man and woman.

In the event of dissolution of a marriage the necessary protection of the children shall be assured.

Parents have the duty to be concerned with the education of their children, to prepare them for socially useful work, and to educate them as proper members of the society. Children are obligated to help and aid their parents.

35. Every child has the right, without any discrimination, to the means of protection that their condition as a minor requires, both on the part of the family as well as the society and the state.

Parents have the same responsibilities toward children born out of wedlock as toward children born within it. All personal characterizations with regard to the nature of one's filial legitimacy are prohibited. The right to investigate paternity is established.

36. The state shall adopt special measures for the protection and assistance of children and adolescents, without any discrimination for reasons of legitimacy or any other condition. Children and adolescents are to be protected against any kind of economic or social exploitation. Employment of children or adolescents in jobs that are damaging to their health or morals, that endanger life, or that can prejudice normal development or the schedule of mandatory schooling, is prohibited.

37. The state shall concede special protection to mothers during an adequate period of time before and after giving birth. During this period, mothers who work must be given time off with pay, and with adequate provision of social security.

The working mother shall have the right to have her minor children cared for by the state while she is at her place of work.

38. The state recognizes the fundamental right of Nicaraguans to be protected against hunger, and shall set forth programs for:

(1) Infant nutrition.

(2) Eradication of chronic malnutrition, assuring adequate availability of food and the equitable distribution thereof.

(3) Nutritional education, aimed at improving the diet through information about the principles of nutrition.

39. Nicaraguans have the right to enjoy the highest levels of physical and mental health. The state has an obligation to adopt measures to achieve:

(1) A reduction in mortality at birth and in infant mortality, as well as the healthy development of children.

(2) Improvement, in all aspects, of occupational health and of the environment.

(3) Prevention, treatment, and eradication of epidemic and endemic diseases, along with occupational and other ailments.

(4) Creation of conditions to assure everyone medical aid and services in the event of illness.

(5) Intensive and systematic development of sports through the creation of all types of facilities.

Section III: Cultural Rights

40. (1) Every person has the right to an education.

(2) Primary and secondary instruction shall be free, obligatory, and accessible to all. Basic education must be promoted for those persons who have not received or finished their primary instruction. Secondary education shall include technical and professional instruction, with the aim of preparing every person for skilled work and providing to all an understanding of Nicaraguan reality. There shall be a close relationship between education and work.

Higher education must also be made equally available to all, based on the capabilities of each person, by the appropriate means and in particular through the continuing establishment of free instruction.

(3) The elimination of illiteracy is declared to be of social interest and is the responsibility of all Nicaraguans.

(4) The freedom of parents to choose for their children schools or colleges different from those established by the state shall be respected, so long as those institutions satisfy the minimum norms prescribed or approved by the state regarding teaching materials, and adhere strictly to the national educational plans.

The right of individuals or entities to establish and direct teaching institutions shall be respected, on the condition they meet the requirements outlined in the preceding paragraph.

The state shall have supervision over all educational centers in the country. This supervision shall be carried out consistently so as to assure compliance with state educational policy and the national plans and programs of studies.

(5) The fees to be charged by private schools shall be approved by the state. In no case shall centers of learning be operated for profit.

(6) The state is obligated to guarantee meals at school, clothing, shoes, school supplies, and school books for all children who need them.

41. Academic freedom and freedom for research are guaranteed as essential principles of education in all spheres.

Educational, administrative, and economic autonomy are guaranteed to the National Autonomous University of Nicaragua (UNAN), in order that it may respond to the needs of the transformation of the country, within the national development plans. The state shall provide UNAN with the necessary economic support to develop a creative curriculum and scientific research adequate to the national reality.

42. In order to coordinate all higher education in the country, there shall be a National Council for Post-Secondary Education, comprising all the institutions on this level, and presided over by the Ministry of Education.

43. The National Autonomous University of Nicaragua shall be the only facility acting in the name of the state to decide on the recognition of diplomas and titles of higher education granted by foreign institutions. The law shall establish standards for the professional accreditation of Nicaraguan nationals and foreigners who have graduated from foreign institutions, on the basis of reciprocity in accordance with the international agreements regarding such matters.

44. The state shall take exclusive charge of the training of preschool and primary-school teachers. The training of teachers for secondary education shall also be a priority task of the state.

45. All persons have the right to participate in cultural life, and to enjoy the benefits of scientific progress and its

applications. The state shall respect the indispensable freedom for scientific research and creative activity. It shall guarantee protection of the moral and material interests of persons engaged in the production of scientific, literary, or artistic works.

46. The state shall have an obligation to adopt necessary measures for the preservation, development, and dissemination of science and culture, which should be oriented toward the full development of the human personality and its sense of dignity, the strengthening of respect for human rights, and the transformation of Nicaraguan society.

The historic, cultural, and artistic heritage of the nation shall be protected by the state by means of the necessary laws.

Title IV: Final Dispositions

47. No provision of this statute shall be construed as conceding to the state, to a group, or to an individual, any right to undertake and carry on activities or commit illegal acts which tend to suppress any of the rights and freedoms recognized herein, or restrict them more than stipulated herein.

Excepted are legal measures aimed at punishing crimes committed, or at the recovery of goods stolen or acquired illegally, under the dictatorial Somoza regime.

48. The exercise of the rights and freedoms of each person is inseparable from the fulfillment of his or her duties to the community.

49. In exceptional situations or cases of emergency which endanger the life or the stability of the nation, such as international or civil wars or the danger of the outbreak thereof; because of public disasters or wars; and for reasons of public order and security of the state, the Junta of the Government of National Reconstruction may adopt provisions which suspend, in part or all of the national territory, the rights and guarantees set forth in this statute. Such suspension may be imposed for a limited period of time, subject to extension in accordance with the prevailing situation in the country.

The provisions of this article do not authorize any

suspension of the rights and guarantees set forth in the following articles: Article 6; Article 7 in regard to servitude; Article 12, paragraph 1; Article 14; Article 17, paragraph 1; Article 19; and Article 26.

50. All persons whose rights or liberties, as recognized in this statute or in the Fundamental Statute promulgated July 20, 1979, have been violated, may seek legal redress in conformity with the law.

Title V: Temporary Dispositions

51. For persons under investigation for crimes specified in the Penal Code and in international conventions, committed during the Somoza regime, the exercise of the rights and guarantees set forth in this statute is suspended for a period of sixty days beginning today.

This suspension does not affect the rights and guarantees listed in Article 49 of this statute.

52. This statute shall go into effect today, from the time of its publication by any means of collective communication, and shall also be published later in the official daily.

*   *   *

Issued in the city of Managua on the twenty-first day of the month of August, 1979, *Year of National Liberation.*

> *Violeta B. de Chamorro*
> *Alfonso Robelo Callejas*
> *Sergio Ramírez Mercado*
> *Moisés Hassan Morales*
> *Daniel Ortega Saavedra*

The Triumph of
Nicaraguan Independence

by Fidel Castro

Heroic Sandinista fighters, comrades of the party and government leadership, people of Holguín, compatriots:

Two weeks ago we thought that in this rally various topics would be discussed, among them the successes and the merits of this province; the enormous transformation to be seen throughout the province and the city; its tremendous march forward and its progress, its new buildings, its new factories, its work spirit, its production successes.

The great merit of having produced 764,000 tons of sugar in this year's harvest: 150,000 tons more than last year, bringing this year's national sugar production to 7,992,000 tons, 96 base, only 8,000 tons short of the eight million mark and surpassing last year's production figure by more than half a million tons. And all this under adverse weather conditions and working the sugar mills right up until yesterday, which was when the last one was stopped.

This is what we were thinking. But when we learned less than forty-eight hours ago that our people were to receive an extraordinary honor, that a large contingent of fighters, of heroic and self-sacrificing leaders, leaders of the sister people of Nicaragua, wished to be with us on this July 26, I realized that today's rally would inevitably turn into a Sandinista rally.

What should we talk about, what else could we talk about, what more extraordinary event of our times, what act of greater historical importance, of greater significance and implications has taken place in recent times than the victory of the Sandinistas in Nicaragua? What has touched us more deeply, what has captured our attention more during these weeks, what could have excited or inspired us more than this popular and heroic victory?

And what greater honor could we have received, what greater splendor for this revolutionary day of ours, what greater honor for this city and this province than the warm, fraternal visit of solidarity from this contingent of heroic, valiant, intelligent, and capable commanders and fighters of the Sandinista National Liberation Front of Nicaragua?

I say solidarity, because we too need solidarity; I say stimulating, because we also need that stimulation. Solidarity, stimulation, because for a long time it was almost a crime to visit Cuba; for a long time imperialism tried to cut the ties with our sister peoples of Latin America and the Caribbean, and for a long time blockaded us, prohibited and thwarted the coming together and development of the natural, historical, and logical ties between the Nicaraguan and the Cuban peoples.

For so many years we have remembered and mourned those brothers of ours who died fighting at Playa Girón [Bay of Pigs], because of the invasion that left precisely from Nicaraguan territory, in one of the most infamous services which the tyrant offered imperialism, given that this same Somoza—now but a shadow of his former self—was the head of the General Staff of the Nicaraguan army at the time of Girón, when the B-26 bombers left from there to bomb our homes, to kill peasant families, women and children, to drop tons of bombs on our militia and soldiers.

How can we fail to see in this gesture of the Sandinistas, in this spontaneous gesture . . . Because it was not our initiative, since we know the tremendous amount of work they have at this moment, the enormous job they have to do, the great need for their presence in the country, especially in these early days. We would not have been able to ask them for this honor, this immense, infinite honor that came entirely from them.

This is proof of the political valor of Sandinismo, proof of revolutionary valor, because we know this world of ours and we know that political and revolutionary valor do not always abound.

They were not prejudiced, they were not afraid. They

didn't have to ask anyone for permission to come to Cuba. They did not have to explain themselves to anyone, nor worry about what anyone would think.

This is proof of political honesty, because they don't go about pretending; they don't go about denying that they are friends of Cuba, that they feel respect for Cuba, that they are in solidarity with Cuba. They are open, they don't harbor fears.

For this reason, I believe that they inspire confidence not only in our people but in all peoples and in world political opinion. They are not prejudiced, in spite of the gossip, the intrigues, the fact that now the campaigns will begin, that now the accusations will begin, once the victory honeymoon has ended.

They do not harbor prejudices, because they are not afraid of the Nicaraguan and Cuban revolutions being confused, because they are way beyond those prejudices.

Yet they themselves will by no means say that the two revolutions are exactly alike. They are both profound revolutions, alike in many ways and in many ways different, as all true revolutions must be.

This is important for our people, important also for world opinion. Every country has its own road, its own problems, its own style, methods, objectives. We have our own; they have theirs. We did things one way, our way; they will do things their way. Similarities: they achieved victory by means similar to ours; we both achieved victory by the only means by which we could free ourselves from imperialist tyranny and domination: gun in hand, fighting fiercely, heroically.

And we should say, we should stress, that the Nicaraguan revolution was noted for its heroism, for its perseverance, for the tenacity of its fighters, because it is not the victory of one day; it is the victory of twenty years of struggle, twenty years of struggle!

Because in the same year that our revolution triumphed, there were already groups of fighters led by that extraordinary and marvelous fighter Carlos Fonseca Amador, follower of Sandino and founder of the Sandinista National Liberation Front, the people's guide in those terrible days when victory was so far away, leader fallen in the struggle, as so many fell in our own land; like Martí, Maceo, Agramonte; like Abel and Frank País from our generation, who fell without being able to see the victory but certain that victory would be achieved!

The young fighters took up Fonseca's struggle. Yes, it was said that the average age of the fighters was twenty years; but the leaders, what's their average age? Some of the oldest are in their thirties—those who began to fight when they were only fifteen, sixteen, seventeen years old, and who faced the difficulties and obstacles for twenty years. Twenty years to gather the fruits of the seed sown, cultivated, and irrigated with blood for such a long time, to achieve victory in the midst of a truly popular epic.

Who among us has not seen—at the movies, on television, in books and magazines—pictures of the incredibly brutal repression, the ruthless, genocidal, unscrupulous war unleashed against the people of Nicaragua by the Somoza dictatorship?

Who has not seen pictures of mothers weeping for their children, for their loved ones; pictures of children crying for their parents, of homes that have been destroyed, of piles of corpses, of torture, murders, bombings of the cities?

Where else has such barbarism been seen? Where else has there been an air force dedicated to dropping tons and tons of bombs on the cities of its own country? On Managua, Masaya, León, Estelí, on this group of martyred cities.

They did not hesitate to give orders to drop 500-pound bombs on populated and even overpopulated areas, acts that really filled the world with anger and amazement and that, in their own way, contributed to creating the huge campaign and the unshakable feeling of solidarity with the Nicaraguan people and the Sandinista fighters.

These are the fruits of imperialist intervention in Nicaragua. These were the fruits of intervention, the bitter fruits of imperialist policy in our hemisphere. Because they were the ones who shaped, aided, and abetted those sanguinary, repressive, reactionary, tyrannical, fascist regimes in this hemisphere.

And it is said, it has been said—and I think even Somoza himself said it—that in the United Nations the government of Somoza never once failed to vote with the government of the United States.

Throughout the world, U.S. policy was to create this type of political regime, throughout the entire world! Not only in our America, but in each and every continent!

As for the bombings, we see similar cases: the bombings of the Namibian camps by the racist South Africans, the Rhodesian racists' bombings of the refugee camps of the people of Zimbabwe, using the most modern planes, the most deadly weapons, sophisticated bombs that spread thousands of pellets that are often not even made of steel, but of rubber, so that surgeons can't spot them in X rays.

Examples of this kind are the genocidal acts perpetrated against the Palestinian people in the Middle East, the constant bombings against the Palestinian camps in Lebanon, against Lebanese communities in Lebanon, bombed practically every day by Israeli planes, symbols of crime.

But it was not only the Israeli bombs falling on the Palestinians, the Lebanese, the imperialist bombs falling on the Namibians and the Zimbabweans; it was also the imperialist bombs, Israeli bombs, falling on the Nicaraguans.

When the imperialists wanted to pretend that they were not furnishing arms, they furnished them through their allies. And who is going to believe that the Israeli state would have sent Somoza those arms, those Galil guns, those bombs, those planes without the consent of and approval of the government of the United States? And with those bombs and guns tens of thousands of people in that country were murdered; we were told that 40,000 people died, that is to say, twice the number of people attending the rally this afternoon.

These are the fruits of the conspiracy that led to the cowardly murder of Sandino, to the implantation of that disgraceful regime that governed the country for almost fifty years and that has disappeared thanks to the heroic struggle of the Nicaraguan people and the Sandinista fighters.

From now on, the people of Nicaragua will also be able to meet together as we have done since our revolution; I also think that one day, in squares such as this one, the portraits and images of the heroes mentioned here by Commander Humberto Ortega will appear alongside the people, ennobling and dignifying revolutionary rallies, and depicted there will undoubtedly be Sandino, Fonseca, and all the patriots that over 150 years—as has been said here—fought for the independence of Nicaragua.

The Sandinista victory is not only a victory over forty-five years of Somocismo; it is a victory over 150 years of foreign domination in the country, it is a victory over many centuries of conquest, exploitation, and foreign domination. If anything is certain it is that for the first time, for the first time in all their history, the Nicaraguan people became completely free and independent on July 19, when the columns of hardened Sandinista forces entered Managua, because our peoples—and especially Central America, which became a hunting ground for pirates, filibusters, and interventionists—had passed from Spanish to Yankee domination.

So that day not only marks the day of the victory of the revolution, but also of the triumph of Nicaraguan independence, two great and important historical objectives achieved in one battle. It is in this that we see the importance and the significance of the victorious conclusion of the struggle led by the Sandinista National Liberation Front.

But this Sandinista victory, this struggle, means even more. A great degree of international solidarity developed around this struggle, and a great degree of unity in all the Central American and Latin American left; around the Sandinista struggle what we could call a great democratic, pro-independence, and anti-interventionist front developed tacitly in Latin America, something of historic significance and enormous importance.

In Latin America and the Caribbean, in this hemisphere, the Sandinista movement encouraged the pro-independence and anti-interventionist feelings of the Latin American peoples. This reached its high point, its moment of culmination, at the last meeting of the Organization of American States. Let's refer to this organization for the first time without adding any epithets, because for the first time, for the first time, there was outright insubordination on the part of the Latin American states.

This is very symptomatic, since the most reactionary and aggressive sectors in the United States advised the present U.S. administration to pursue a policy of intervention in Nicaragua, and at this meeting the United States advocated an inter-American peace-keeping force, supposedly to bring peace to Nicaragua, when peace in

Nicaragua, the peace imposed by imperialism since it began its many interventions and set up that reactionary regime, was the peace of the grave. In reality this was the kind of peace they wanted to continue upholding in order to prevent revolutionary peace, to prevent the Sandinista victory, to deprive the people of their victory.

We know what these inter-American peace-keeping forces amount to, who supplies the weapons, who leads them, who supplies them, and who makes up their forces. We have seen these so-called inter-American forces more than once before.

The imperialist aim was really a sinister one: it was to intervene in Nicaragua. The imperialists were used to having all the Latin American governments say yes, but this time a sufficient number of Latin American governments said no!

And, as always, the pretexts were very noble: "to bring peace to the suffering people of Nicaragua." They did not want this moment to come, they did not want the nineteenth of July to come. A month later the Sandinistas brought real peace, the peace of a happy and victorious people; a people that had suffered to the full, true, but a people that was also full of hope and optimism in the future.

We, our people, cannot help but note the full magnitude and significance of this historic event: the defeat of the U.S. interventionist scheme in the heart of the Latin American states. There was a majority which resolutely opposed intervention and defended the principle of nonintervention, of sovereignty, of absolute respect for the sovereignty of our peoples, as something sacred.

It must be said that the U.S. proposal was isolated. In the end they adopted an intelligent position. If they had voted in favor of their own proposal, that is, in favor of the proposal for intervention, they would have ended up in the company of Paraguay and Somoza, because the only one who advocated intervention, who openly voted for intervention, was Somoza, and I think Paraguay as well.

Of course, intervention was in Somoza's interest, for the time being at least. Such a course would have preserved the National Guard and would have preserved his interests, along with those of the monopolies. If the United States had abstained, it would have found itself together with Chile, Uruguay, El Salvador, and Guatemala, and they did not think it was very honorable to be seen in that kind of company. And so they too voted with the majority. An interesting phenomenon.

In our opinion the decision, the result of the meeting, constituted a great victory for the people of our America and it helped develop the spirit of solidarity with Nicaragua. And in the position maintained at the OAS, we must stress the role of Panama, Costa Rica, Venezuela and the other Andean Pact countries, and that of Mexico, Jamaica, Grenada, and others. In the creation of this democratic, anti-interventionist front which has formed, we must mention the names of people as well as countries: the names of Torrijos, Carazo, López Portillo, Manley, and Bishop. And it is also only fair to recall the name of a person who, though he is no longer president of his country, contributed a great deal to the development of this solidarity with the Sandinista struggle: the former president of Venezuela, Carlos Andrés Pérez.

And let me stress that there was not a single party or organization of the left in Latin America that did not express its willingness to struggle; not a single one failed to express its solidarity with the struggle of the Sandinista people.

It is very important for all the peoples still suffering from fascism and the bloodiest tyrannies that this climate, this front, and this spirit should be maintained. This is a duty—in our opinion—of the Sandinistas as well; it will be their contribution, the contribution of the victorious people of Nicaragua, toward maintaining that spirit and that broad front.

Many questions are now being raised, and there are many people wanting to establish similarities between what happened in Cuba and what has happened in Nicaragua.

Some of these questions are not being posed in good faith, inspired by the wish to start creating justifications and seeking pretexts to apply aggressive measures against the people of Nicaragua as well, blockades against the people of Nicaragua, aggression against the people of Nicaragua—all those filthy measures and all those crimes they committed against us—and we must be careful about this.

The Nicaraguans have given a magnificent answer for those people with this sort of aim in mind who have made assertions or expressed fears to the effect that Nicaragua would become a new Cuba. The Nicaraguans have replied: No, Nicaragua will become a new Nicaragua! And this is something quite different.

They do not see themselves in us, as if they were looking in a mirror. Rather, it is we who today see ourselves mirrored in them, because nothing reminds us more of our own struggles, our sacrifices, and our own image in those early days of the revolution.

No two revolutions are the same. They can't be. There are many similarities—as I said—as to spirit, heroism, combat. But our problems are not exactly the same as their problems; the conditions under which our revolution took place are not exactly the same as the conditions under which their revolution is taking place, including the fact that in our case this front I mentioned did not exist and that the imperialists launched their campaigns and their aggressions immediately.

The imperialists knew less then, and now even the imperialists have managed to learn something. Not much, but something.

The conditions under which their struggle was fought, its characteristics, were different. For instance, the unity of the entire people, which was an essential condition for victory, the participation of all social strata, the organization of various popular movements, which joined ranks, reaching certain compromises, creating certain circumstances that differed from ours. In other words, in Nicaragua and Cuba things are not going to be exactly the same, quite the contrary.

Some of the characteristics we have noted in our Nicaraguan revolutionary comrades are worthy of mention. Firstly, the people's militant spirit, their heroism, their bravery. They have distinguished themselves as great fighters, but they have also distinguished themselves as great political tacticians and strategists. They have displayed great wisdom, great ability to unite, great ability to act in difficult, complex circumstances.

They fought heroically, but they have also been able to be flexible and when they needed to negotiate in a certain way to avoid the risks of intervention, they were not afraid to negotiate. And they showed great ability, great talent both in military and political strategy. Needless to say, had it been otherwise their victory would have been inexplicable.

Even during the final stage, when the Somoza regime was in its death throes, they discussed how the end would be, the graveside protocol, as it were, Somoza's funeral. Several countries took part in these talks, the Government of National Reconstruction took part, the Sandinista leadership took part, and even the United States took part.

And as *Granma* briefly explained, Somoza's demise was supposed to occur at four in the morning; then somebody called Urcuyo—at first I found it hard to remember the name, even now I do not remember it very well, and I daresay in a couple of weeks I will have forgotten it again—then somebody called Urcuyo was supposed to take over at eight in the morning and finally hand over the government to the Junta of National Reconstruction at one in the afternoon. In the interim period I believe that someone was to be appointed head of the National Guard, something like that.

The Sandinistas made some concessions. And it was wise of them to make these concessions, those they thought they should make. At the same time they were firm and did not make concessions they should not have made.

It was assumed, of course, that there would be a new army. The country could not remain in the hands of those genocidal maniacs. Basically, the new army would be made up of the Sandinista fighters and, it is said, also some National Guard members who were not guilty of corruption, repression, and crimes.

Now, this may be all right in principle, in theory, but it is hard to imagine there could be even one of them who was not guilty of corruption, repression, and crimes. However the Sandinista attitude was a generous one.

We were too, in our own struggle. We repeatedly appealed to the army. At the end we even held talks with them, and they said to us: "We've lost the war, how do we bring it to an end?"

We gave them our opinion on how to proceed. We told them that the forces in Santiago should surrender and that they should neither discuss things with the U.S. embassy, nor stage a coup d'etat in the capital, nor help Batista escape. And so we came to an agreement. We waited for the thirty-first [of December 1958] and we did not attack the Santiago garrison, waiting for the agreement to be honored.

But they did the exact opposite; they staged a coup in Havana, they came to an agreement with the U.S. embassy, and they saw Batista off at the airport. So that was the end of the agreement and we had no choice but to disarm the army, which we did in forty-eight hours, as you all know perfectly well, so there is no need to repeat it here.

Well, something similar happened in Nicaragua; when this Urcuyo character had been appointed president, he said no, he intended to stay there until 1981. So the Sandinistas gave the order to attack, and in less than seventy-two hours they disarmed the National Guard, and now there is no National Guard. It turned out that the U.S. government could not even honor its own part in the agreements.

Nonetheless, the Government of National Reconstruction and the Sandinista leadership have done a very correct thing, in our opinion, in maintaining the generous attitude they displayed in these talks. Of course, the U.S. government was not concerned about the tens of thousands of people killed by the bombings; but they were very concerned about the lives of Somoza's thugs, his poor little thugs. But the magnanimity and generosity displayed by the Sandinistas has been extraordinary, exemplary, exemplary!

Needless to say all this was just to pave the way for launching a campaign against the Sandinista movement, which has won so much solidarity and sympathy all over the world.

And so the Sandinistas have not only been heroic and efficient in war and flexible in politics; they have also been extraordinarily magnanimous in victory! I am sure that this will earn the broadest sympathy and will strengthen feelings of solidarity throughout the world. It will deprive the reactionaries of arguments, it will deprive them of weapons, it will deprive them of fuel for slander and defamation.

It also shows the enormous influence the Sandinista commanders and the Government of National Reconstruction have over the masses, because the masses have not forgotten—nor will they ever forget—the crimes, torture, and bombings. They will not forget. But they have also given proof of their great trust in the leadership by holding back when it was necessary for them to hold back.

We hope that in Nicaragua's case the imperialists will not repeat their interventionist ventures or try fostering counterrevolution. Of course, we are not going to deceive ourselves. We're not going to imagine that the reactionaries will leave the Nicaraguan revolution in peace, despite its magnanimity, generous attitude, and democratic aims.

They have said that if an election is needed it's fine with them to have an election. In any election held in Nicaragua, no matter how many resources are supplied to the reactionary bands, the Sandinistas will win with an enormous majority.

In any kind of election, under any kind of constitution where the citizen has the right to vote and the citizen does vote, the Sandinistas would win.

This is why—and this is what I'm explaining to our people—it's the circumstances in which the Nicaraguan victory was won that determine that the ways they adopt differ from ours. Furthermore, the fact that right now Nicaragua is in ruins, completely destroyed, calls for a national reconstruction program with the participation of every sector of Nicaraguan society.

The Sandinistas are revolutionaries. We don't deny it, nobody denies it, they don't deny it. But they are not extremists, they are realists. And it is realists who make the best revolutions, the best and most profound revolutions.

I predict that they will go far because they are taking their time, because they're not extremists, because they're taking things slowly. They know what to aim for at each stage of a political and revolutionary process and the means that correspond to these aims. I'm sure of that.

They used their heads, too, the Sandinistas, because they closed ranks at just the right moment and the result was victory, fruit of the wisdom with which they acted. And our greatest hope is that this unity becomes ever more solid and closer as an essential requisite for the future. The people, weapons, unity. That's all they need to go as far as they want for as long as they want.

They are now faced with a tremendous job, tremendous,

much worse than the one that faced us when we won; because our war, and the development of the columns and the guerrilla fronts, was different. They combined the development of the columns and the guerrilla fronts with insurrection in the cities, an infallible system that neither Somoza nor the National Guard could beat.

The enemy had no qualms at all in shelling and bombing the rebellious cities with every available weapon, mercilessly destroying entire cities and facilities of all kinds and leaving behind an enormous wake of destruction, the country's finances bankrupt with not a single reserve left.

Engineer Alfonso Robelo was telling me that there were some $3 million left in the treasury, with an immediate debt of $250 million and an overall foreign debt of $1,200 million. There wasn't a single cent left. Therefore one of the first things they had to do was nationalize the banks, among other things, as a measure to protect depositors from ruin, because the banks were bankrupt and nobody could guarantee the savings held in them.

So that's one of the first measures they've had to take. There's much hunger in Nicaragua. I believe that Nicaragua needs help from everybody. In the past few weeks, a large number of leaders have expressed their readiness to help Nicaragua.

I think that's very good.

Governments of different hues, of different ideologies, of different political systems, have expressed their readiness to assist the people of Nicaragua on a large scale. And Nicaragua certainly needs this help.

Even the United States has stated that it's ready to send food and organize other kinds of help. We're glad to hear it. They said they were going to start an airlift and send 300 tons of food a day. We think that's a very good idea.

Martí said that heaven wanted tyrants to be wise only once. Needless to say, Somoza wasn't wise even once; the government of the United States, however, has been wise at least on this one occasion, because it's much better in every sense, more productive, and makes for better relations among the peoples and for a climate of peace all over the world, to send food instead of sending bombs and marines, like they did in Vietnam and so many other places.

Naturally—since I mentioned Vietnam—if the United States had intervened in Nicaragua it would have been an act of suicide for United States policy in this hemisphere, because we haven't the slightest doubt that the Sandinistas would have continued fighting in spite of U.S. intervention. There's no question about that.

We're extremely happy that it didn't happen—who knows how many lives have been spared for that very reason—but we are also convinced that had there been an intervention it would have met with tremendous resistance on the part of Sandino's people. And not only that, but also that a gigantic Vietnam might have developed throughout Central America and in the rest of Latin America, a gigantic Vietnam.

Intervention would have been an act of sheer stupidity, but also an act that would have meant a great deal of bloodshed for our peoples.

So an intervention in Nicaragua wouldn't have gone unpunished, of course—we must be quite clear about that—but we are glad that the firm struggle waged by the people of Nicaragua, international solidarity, the support given by the Latin American peoples, and the realism and flexibility of the Sandinistas prevented the perpetration of one of the most mistaken acts imaginable, and which was a real possibility.

We are glad to know the United States is sending food to Nicaragua. We are glad to know that everybody is sending food and giving aid of all kinds to the people of Nicaragua.

We are not rich; we cannot compete with the United States in numbers of planes and tons of food. But we will send something, because even though we are poor we can always spare some of what we have.

And something very important: we may not have great financial or material resources, but we do have human resources.

Engineer Robelo said here that they need doctors, that they need campaigns to wipe out illiteracy. And we know our doctors and teachers. They'll go wherever they're needed. If they have to go to the mountains, they go to the mountains; if to the countryside, the countryside. In Cuba and in Ethiopia, in Vietnam, in Yemen, in Angola, anywhere.

Nicaragua is much nearer, right nearby. There's practically the same distance between Cape San Antonio and Managua as between Cape San Antonio and Maisí Point. So it's really close.

Therefore, I believe that we are expressing the feelings of our party and of our people when we say to our Nicaraguan brothers and sisters that, if they plan to put into effect a broad health and medical care program and there aren't enough Nicaraguan doctors, we are ready to send all the doctors they need to support this health program.

Of course, we do have more than one thousand doctors working abroad, but we still have some to spare. We have our commitments and we can meet them.

How would we be able to do it? By asking our hospitals and our doctors for their collaboration. We have done it on other occasions, for example, in the matter of time off following guard duty. We've said wait for the future, a splendid future because some four thousand students are already entering medical school every year and we are building medical schools in practically every province. We would need the collaboration of the hospitals, People's Power [elected legislative assemblies], the public health sector, and especially the doctors themselves, to cover the work of those who go.

We've already sent the first medical brigade of sixty people, forty of them doctors. It was done quickly, in a matter of hours.

We sent a large medical brigade when Nicaragua was hit by an earthquake, even though Somoza was still there. And I remember that the colonel they mentioned today, who wasn't yet a colonel at the time, that son of Somoza's who they say was the head of the EBI [Basic Infantry Training School], was waiting at the airport to steal the shipments that came in.

So they stole the medicines we sent. They couldn't steal our doctors, however, and our doctors did a good job, offered their services to the people, and the people were very friendly toward them. If we did it when Somoza was there, we can certainly do it now.

We have doctors now and we'll have more in the future. But we're not going to wait for those. The ones we send will come from those we have now.

If our doctors collaborate—and of course I'm sure they will—if our hospitals, the heads of hospitals, the health sectors, everybody collaborates, we can find all the doctors we need to tell the people of Nicaragua that we will send them all they need if they haven't enough themselves.

This means that if they need 100, we'll send them 100. If they need 200, we'll send them 200. And if they need as many as 500, we'll send them 500. No trouble at all.

The need for a large-scale education campaign has also been mentioned here. And it looks as if there are some teachers here who are quite enthusiastic at the idea. A great educational campaign.

Only a revolutionary government can carry out a great health and education campaign. Who knows how many lives they will save, especially how many children's lives they will save, with campaigns against polio, tetanus, and tuberculosis.

Many lives are going to be saved in just a few years. In fact, many lives are going to be saved in but a few weeks. I know how much people appreciate a health campaign; I know how much people appreciate an educational campaign.

Even in the midst of destruction and ruins, a revolutionary government can wage a great campaign in these fields, and since our country has plenty of experience in these things we can offer some advice in both the health and the education campaigns. And, I repeat, if they don't have enough teachers in Nicaragua to put this education campaign into effect, we are ready to send them as many as they need.

It's not for nothing that we have more than 30,000 students in our primary education teacher training schools, and tens of thousands—50,000 I think—training as teachers in the pedagogical institutions. We're doing all right.

We also know that our teachers go wherever they are sent—to the most remote places, to the farthest mountains, to the most forgotten little town.

They're not interested in being in the capital. We know our teachers and our doctors and we know how much they can do. This is why our country can make quite a valuable contribution in these two fields.

Needless to say, we are also ready to collaborate, within the scope of our modest resources, in any other field.

It is not a case of our going to engage in politics in

Nicaragua—and there will certainly be some who will say that we are.

Who's going to engage in politics, who's going to influence the Sandinistas? On the contrary, our teachers and our doctors will be influenced by the Sandinista spirit, and we are very pleased and happy about this. The revolutionary spirit of the Sandinistas will have a great effect on them. Everyone knows our technicians' dedication to their work.

I repeat that we're glad that the United States and other countries are to help Nicaragua. What's more, we're ready to enter an emulation campaign with the United States, an emulation campaign to see who can do the most for Nicaragua. We invite the United States, we invite all the countries of Latin America, we invite all the countries of Europe, the countries of the Third World, our sister socialist nations, everybody, to take part in an emulation campaign to help Nicaragua. This is our position, in order to make a really human, really constructive effort based on a spirit of emulation.

Of course, when I mentioned who could do the most you all stood up. What do you think? What do you think? [*Shouts of "Yes!"*] And that we're willing and ready to do it? [*Shouts of "Yes!"*] Then, we ask you to raise your hands, on behalf of all our people, as an expression of this feeling of solidarity with the people of Nicaragua. [*All hands go up.*] Our feelings, our response couldn't be otherwise.

The Sandinistas have set a further example of how much a revolutionary spirit can accomplish. Weak men never achieve any goals; timid souls never get anywhere. But a revolutionary spirit can achieve even the most incredible goals.

We thank the Sandinistas not only for their beautiful gesture, their unforgettable gesture, for the great honor they have conferred on us with their presence and their affectionate and fraternal words. We also thank them for stimulating us in our own efforts, in our own struggle, because they help us to improve, to overcome our own shortcomings.

They stimulate us in our task of perfecting our work, perfecting our revolution, in the uncompromising struggle against weaknesses, against errors, against things badly done; this struggle is not a temporary campaign, a matter of one day, one week, one month, or one year but rather a struggle that we must go on waging for many years.

Now they are faced by the problem that all those who begin a process on the ruins of their country must face, while here, with twenty years of revolution behind us, the conditions are different, the circumstances are different.

What better way to celebrate this July 26, to pay tribute to our martyrs, what better way to honor our visitors than for every one of us to promise and commit ourselves to make more of an effort, to struggle harder, to work harder, to become better!

Long live the revolutionary victory in Nicaragua!

Long live Sandino!

Long live the FSLN!

Long live the Government of National Reconstruction of Nicaragua!

Long live the friendship and solidarity between the peoples of Nicaragua and Cuba!

Patria o Muerte!

Venceremos!

APPENDIX

Imperialism Launches Propaganda Drive Against Sandinistas

by Barry Sheppard and Mary-Alice Waters

The imperialist enemies of the revolution in Nicaragua have opened a concerted international campaign to pressure the Sandinista leadership not to carry the revolution beyond bourgeois limits, and to undercut the development of international solidarity with this revolution by the world working-class movement.

A series of articles has appeared in major capitalist dailies in the United States, Europe, and Latin America, all of which put forward the same basic line: The Nicaraguan revolution is threatened by "extremists" on the left; the new government realizes that it can't go too far too fast with radical measures or they will not receive sufficient foreign aid to rebuild the country; and the Sandinistas realize that their true allies are the capitalist businessmen of Nicaragua, as represented in the civilian junta that makes up the Government of National Reconstruction.

An article by Marlise Simons carried on the front page of the August 21 *Washington Post,* entitled "Nicaragua Expels Trotskyist Group In Crackdown," begins as follows:

> Despite the revolutionary euphoria of the past month, the first signs of organized opposition to Nicaragua's new government are coming from the extreme left and not, as widely anticipated, from conservative businessmen.
>
> At the same time, the government's first act of political impatience has been to expel some 60 Latin American Trotskyists

74

whom it charged with being "counterrevolutionaries" and "creating problems for the Sandinista revolution."

Although the government is anxious not to disappoint popular expectations of change, it seems determined to resist extremist pressure for sudden, radical measures that could frighten both the domestic and foreign private sectors and retard economic reconstruction.

Along a similar line, an article by Richard J. Meislin in the August 20 issue of the *New York Times* states:

In Managua, the perception that the Sandinista military leadership, and not the five highest members of the civilian junta, was running the country, which was prevalent in diplomatic circles and among some junta members themselves only two weeks ago, has virtually disappeared.

The Simons article makes clear that this is the line Washington thinks is most effective right now in applying pressure against the Nicaraguan revolution. She explains that "some U.S. diplomats here agree that several reports in the U.S. media have been 'irresponsible,' or 'distorting the truth.' This applies, they say, to clichés about 'the new Cuba' and 'rising anti-Americanism.'"

The "responsible" attitude the U.S. State Department wants to promote is to warn the Sandinista fighters who led the revolution that *they had better* leave the civilian junta in command of the government; that "conservative businessmen" are the mainstay of the revolution and left "extremists" are its enemy; that the revolution is a *bourgeois* revolution and must stay within *bourgeois* limits.

In warning of the "extremist" danger to the revolution, both Simons and Meislin are very precise. They point to any measures that "could frighten both the domestic and foreign private sectors." As an example, Meislin singles out the proposal that workers be paid back pay "for the two months the country was at war. It is money the government has promised the workers but that few of the hard-pressed employers have been able to pay."

To make sure that the Sandinistas understand the nature of these warnings, Washington is insisting on political concessions as a precondition for providing desperately needed food, medicine, and other aid. In reserve, they are holding the threat of military intervention, spearheaded by the Somocista National Guard units that were withdrawn to Honduras and El Salvador.

This blackmail of the Sandinistas by Washington was spelled out in the article by Simons:

In recent days, leaders of the Sandinista command and junta members have said privately they fear they may be caught in a vicious circle: they require fast massive foreign assistance to ensure that moderation prevails, yet Western governments appear to be withholding funds until they can be sure they are not financing "a new Cuba."

On August 15, the *New York Times* ran an editorial warning the U.S. Congress not to place obstacles in the way of this blackmail plan. The editorial stated:

No one can say that Nicaragua will not go the Cuban route but it is significant that the junta is pressing for American economic help. The legislation needed to expand American aid programs must pass a Congress in which diehard Somoza supporters command key [congressional] committees. Doubtless they will cite every outburst about "Yankee Imperialism" as proof that Nicaragua is undeserving, in turn confirming the leftist view that America is an implacable antagonist. It will be a test of American maturity to keep extremists on all sides from fulfilling their own dire prophecies.

Confronted with this imperialist campaign and the tremendous devastation of the country wrought by Somoza in the final weeks of the civil war, the Sandinista leadership faces complex, difficult problems in carrying the revolution forward.

The Sandinista National Liberation Front (FSLN) must make it as difficult as possible for the imperialists to be able to refuse to provide food and other aid.

In order to advance the interests of the working masses of Nicaragua, the Sandinistas have taken and must continue to take measures that cut into the profit-making prerogatives of native and foreign capitalists. At the same time they must make it as difficult as possible for the imperialists to respond through military intervention.

The FSLN leadership needs to maintain the masses in arms because of the continuing threat of counterrevolution. But the armed defenders of the revolution need to be a trained, disciplined force, with heavy arms and sophisticated military equipment.

These needs of the revolution present major tactical problems for the revolutionists in the Sandinista command.

The imperialist press, in its warnings to the Sandinista leadership, has utilized a convenient target—a group called the "Simón Bolívar Brigade" (the "Trotskyists" referred to in the headline of the Simons article).

The Simón Bolívar Brigade is an armed international contingent that was initiated by the Partido Socialista de los Trabajadores (PST—Socialist Workers Party) of Colombia in the closing weeks of the Nicaraguan civil war. Individuals associated with the brigade entered Nicaragua only in the final days of the fighting.

Since the fall of the Somoza dictatorship the brigade and a number of other left organizations, including the Maoists, have attempted to utilize the objective problems facing the revolution—the gap between the great hopes of the masses for immediate improvements in their living standards and the difficulties in achieving these goals quickly— to "outflank" the Sandinistas on the left. Their tactic was to try to expose the Sandinista leadership as not being revolutionary enough.

Moreover, even though they were not acting under the direction of the FSLN, they carried out their agitation and activities in the name of the FSLN. Working people who supported the brigade's activities were thus left with the false impression that they were following the FSLN.

The reaction of the FSLN was to initiate several meetings with the brigade leadership to try to convince them of the need to place all armed units under the unified FSLN command and coordinate their activities with those of the FSLN.

The FSLN finally publicly summoned all brigade members to appear at its offices in Managua August 14. In response, the brigade organized a demonstration of some 1,000 persons in front of the FSLN headquarters. They brought people to the demonstration under the pretense that they were going to discuss problems of wages and trade union organization with the FSLN leadership.

Following this provocation, the FSLN ordered non-Nicaraguan members of the brigade out of the country.

Some were expelled, and others are reportedly still being sought inside Nicaragua.

Since the brigade was organized by the Colombian PST, a Trotskyist group that is a sympathizing organization of the Fourth International, the actions of this group gave the bourgeois press a convenient target to launch its campaign against "Trotskyism" in the hopes of sowing confusion among the supporters of the Nicaraguan revolution.

But the Simón Bolívar Brigade is not Trotskyist. No one had to agree with Trotskyism to join the brigade. It was composed of Latin American revolutionists who wanted to help bring down Somoza.

Furthermore, while the Colombian PST is a sympathizing organization of the Fourth International, it did not set up the Simón Bolívar Brigade in consultation with or under the control of the elected leadership bodies of the Fourth International, the world Trotskyist organization. The leaders of the brigade set their own policies without regard to the policies of the Fourth International, and in Nicaragua they have carried out a policy contrary to the position adopted by the United Secretariat of the Fourth International, as expressed in its statement of August 15. The position of the Fourth International is to build a campaign of solidarity with the Nicaraguan revolution in collaboration with the FSLN, not in opposition to it.

Moreover, the Fourth International has always stood on the conviction that revolutions are led by forces that arise out of the living struggle in their own country. It is a grotesque idea that a group of non-Nicaraguans like the Simón Bolívar Brigade could jump into the revolutionary process from the outside and through a series of maneuvers build a counter leadership to the FSLN.

Although the imperialist press has utilized the activities of the Simón Bolívar Brigade for their attack on "extremism," the target is the Nicaraguan revolution itself. This is why papers like the *Washington Post, New York Times, Le Monde,* and other imperialist mouthpieces, not noted for featuring news about Trotskyism, gave top-priority coverage to the expulsion of the brigade leaders from Nicaragua.

The message is clear.

First, the imperialists want to let the FSLN know that any measures the new leadership takes against the capitalists will be considered "extremism" by Washington, and that it will react accordingly.

Second, the goal is to falsely portray the FSLN as bourgeois liberals, or at least as the captives of the bourgeois liberals in the junta. This is designed to disorient inexperienced revolutionists and sow confusion among working-class forces around the world who are hoping to see the FSLN fighters carry their struggle through to the end as did the Cuban leadership.

Third, the campaign against Trotskyism in the bourgeois press is aimed at dividing and weakening the forces that could build an effective international movement in solidarity with the Nicaraguan revolution and the FSLN leaders. By smearing Trotskyism the imperialists hope to place obstacles in the way of the international solidarity campaign that the Fourth International has called for and begun to organize.

In fact, the bourgeois press coverage is attempting to give the impression that there is really no need for such a solidarity campaign: the imperialists are reasonable and will, in the end, provide the necessary aid. Similarly, their "friendly" advice to the FSLN contained in these articles is designed to lull the Nicaraguan people as well as the international workers' movement into thinking there is no real danger of imperialist-backed military attack.

This imperialist propaganda drive against the Sandinistas and the Nicaraguan revolution makes it all the more urgent to mount the broadest possible response from the workers' movement internationally. Massive economic pressure is being brought to bear against the Nicaraguan people, backed by threats of renewed military operations. The trade unions and other organizations of the workers' movement must reach out to students, churches, and all democratic forces, to organize solidarity with the Nicaraguan revolution and demand aid from the imperialist governments with no strings attached.

The Nicaraguan people must be able to feed their hungry, heal their wounded, and rebuild their industry while taking the fate of their country into their own hands.

Further Reading

Books

Cuba for Beginners
By RIUS $3.45
Disaster in Chile
Edited by Les Evans 4.95
Dynamics of the Cuban Revolution
By Joseph Hansen 5.95
Land or Death: The Peasant Struggle in Peru
By Hugo Blanco 3.95
The Leninist Strategy of Party Building: The Debate on Guerrilla Warfare in Latin America
By Joseph Hansen 7.95
Politics of Chicano Liberation
Edited by Olga Rodríguez 3.45
Puerto Ricans in the U.S.
Edited by Catarino Garza 1.95
Selected Speeches of Fidel Castro 4.00

Pamphlets

The Ethiopian Revolution
By Ernest Harsch .85
Fidel Castro's Speech to the United Nations 1.25
Second Declaration of Havana
By Fidel Castro .75
Socialism and Man in Cuba
By Che Guevara .65
Upsurge in Africa:
Cuba, the U.S., and the New Rise of the African Liberation Struggle
By David Frankel .75
Workers and Peasants to Power!
By Hugo Blanco .95

Write for a free catalog

Pathfinder Press 410 West St., New York, N.Y. 10014